Our American Century

Prelude to the Century · 1870-1900

★

By the Editors of Time-Life Books, Alexandria, Virginia

Contents

★

Nation on the Move

★

AMERICA 1870–1900

Celebrating completion of the transcontinental railroad, men and locomotives from east and west meet at Promontory, Utah, on May 10, 1869.

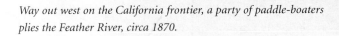

Way out west on the California frontier, a party of paddle-boaters plies the Feather River, circa 1870.

Arching majestically over the East River, the Brooklyn Bridge links Manhattan (foreground) with the still-autonomous city of Brooklyn, circa 1890.

Refusing to give up their traditional life of hunting and raiding, Geronimo's renegade Apaches attend a peace parley in 1886.

Crammed between canyon walls, a crowded boom town goes up in Creede, Colorado, after the discovery of a nearby silver lode in 1890.

No longer a frontier town, San Diego boasted of telephone service, electricity, and the West Coast's first streetcar in 1887.

In Manchester, New Hampshire, the Dow family gathers to celebrate a golden wedding anniversary in 1895.

In 1898, a mule train carries supplies to miners in the Klondike along the border between Alaska and Canada—site of the world's biggest gold rush.

*A New York City trolley laden with commuters rolls
by a billboard plastered with posters, circa 1896.*

Ignoring the pleas of a beggar, Standard Oil founder John D. Rockefeller (center) confers with colleagues in 1880. Although this photograph was used by rivals trying to discredit Rockefeller, he was actually one of the age's most generous philanthropists.

In 1870, Hiram R. Revels of Mississippi became the first African-American elected to the U.S. Senate. A clergyman and educator, Revels served the one year remaining in the unexpired term of the former Confederate president, Jefferson Davis.

Hurtling Headlong to a New Century

Finally relieved of much of the trauma of the Civil War, the nation in 1870 began rushing forward. No clearer sign of this rapid change could be found than in the election of an African American to the U.S. Senate. Hiram R. Revels would fill out the term of none other than Jefferson Davis, who had vacated the position to serve as president of the Confederacy.

Other events pointed to three decades of extraordinary economic growth and vitality. A 30-year-old Cleveland entrepreneur named John D. Rockefeller formed the Standard Oil Company to exploit a new industry—the refining and marketing of kerosene for home lamps. The following year, the Great Fire of 1871 destroyed much of Chicago *(right)*, but the city immediately began rebuilding itself into the nation's second largest metropolis. And as Chicago went, so went the country.

Indeed, the years from 1870 to 1900 proved to be the exhilarating prelude to the triumphs and tragedies of the 20th century. Here already were the themes of industrial growth, urban change, soaring technology, the struggle for equality, and the rise to world power that would characterize the United States in the century to come. "Never, perhaps," wrote historian John A. Garraty, "did the American people display more vigor, more imagination or greater confidence in themselves and the future of their country."

Their land was transformed from an agrarian nation into an industrial colossus. Abundant natural resources yielded the raw materials. Advances in know-how showed the way to better methods. A booming birthrate and

Amid the rubble of the Great Fire of 1871, which destroyed 17,450 buildings and left 100,000 homeless, construction crews begin to rebuild Chicago (right). By 1885, the city was the home of the world's first skyscraper—the 10-story Home Insurance Building.

stepped-up flow of immigrants provided the workers. And the can-do spirit of businessmen like Rockefeller drove the creation of ever-larger enterprises with their enhanced efficiencies of scale.

The full potential for oil awaited the 20th century, but the astonishing story of steel was already unfolding. Thanks to new technology and an innovative method to remove impurities from iron ore, American production soared from 77,000 tons in 1870 to 11.4 million tons in 1900.

Steel provided girders for bridges and skyscrapers *(pages 152-169)* and barbed wire for the rapidly expanding Western cattle ranges. But the industry's best customers were the railroads, which consumed about 60 percent of all steel made in the United States. The network of track nearly quadrupled, reaching 193,000 miles by 1900—40 percent of the world total. The four transcontinental lines completed by 1883 accounted for the most significant mileage, linking coasts 3,000 miles apart and shrinking travel that had taken months by stagecoach or ship to a mere seven days.

Spanning the continent by rail helped make accessible its vast wilderness. In 1872, only three years after the completion of the initial transcontinental railroad, the first national park was established at Yellowstone *(right)*, an area of 3,472 square miles in the future states of Wyoming, Montana, and Idaho. Burgeoning railroads also served the new gold and silver mines of the West, carried eastward the cattle that cowboys drove up from Texas, and ferried west those who sought their fortunes on land provided them free under the Homestead Act of 1862. Relying increasingly on labor-saving machinery such as harvesters and combines, the homesteaders established a million farms west of the Mississippi.

The nation's industrial wares went on display in 1876 at the Philadelphia Centennial Exposition, which celebrated the 100th anniversary of the signing of the Declaration of Independence. In Machinery Hall, viewers could inspect a 1500-horsepower steam engine—the world's biggest and most powerful—but smaller gadgets also at-

Yellowstone National Park was created by Congress in 1872 to preserve this spectacular piece of frontier in Wyoming, Montana, and Idaho. The terraces at Mammoth Hot Springs shown here were formed by minerals deposited by water as it cooled.

"Genius is one percent inspiration and ninety-nine percent perspiration."

Thomas A. Edison

tracted crowds. There was a typewriter on which an attendant would write a letter home for any visitor willing to fork up 50 cents. One of the exposition judges, Emperor Dom Pedro II of Brazil, tried out an even more exotic device. "My God, it talks!" he exclaimed, and dropped the receiver.

What talked, of course, was the telephone. Earlier that year, Alexander Graham Bell had obtained Patent Number 174,465 on the device. Bell came from a Scottish family of teachers and audiologists, and the invention grew out of his work with the deaf. At first, it was considered little more than a novelty—the president of Western Union called it an "electrical toy"—but by the turn of the century Americans would be talking back and forth over more than one million telephones.

Western Union, meanwhile, had quickly recovered its corporate wits and commissioned Thomas A. Edison to work on telephonic transmission. Concerned that the telephone would be too expensive for most people, Edison began tinkering with a "telephone repeater"—a machine that could record a person's spoken message and then be taken to a central switchboard so the words could be transmitted to a designated recipient. In 1877, he hooked up a telephone diaphragm to a stylus that etched grooves in a tin-foil-covered cylinder cranked by hand. He sang "Mary had a little lamb," and to the astonishment of associates at his so-called invention factory in Menlo Park, New Jersey, the machine—the first phonograph—played back his high-pitched voice.

Even more profound in its ramifications for everyday life was Edison's work with electric lighting. In 1879, after heating hundreds of different materials with electricity, he settled upon a filament of carbonized cotton thread and perfected the first practical incandescent light bulb. Three years later, he opened in New York's lower Manhat-

---

Crowds throng Memorial Hall in Philadelphia for the opening of the Centennial Exposition in 1876 (left). The show celebrated a century of progress since the Declaration of Independence.

Using the instrument he patented in 1876, Alexander Graham Bell inaugurates long-distance telephone service between New York and Chicago. It was a far cry from when Bell first telephoned his assistant in the next room: "Mr. Watson, come here; I want you."

Thomas Edison slumps wearily in his "invention factory" in 1888 after working 72 straight hours to perfect a wax-cylinder model of his phonograph. His incandescent light bulb—first demonstrated in 1879—made possible the illumination of the nation's rapidly growing cities.

These steamboats, docked at Bismarck in Dakota Territory in 1877, were the kind piloted and chronicled by the writer Samuel Langhorne Clemens—Mark Twain (right).

tan a commercial power station that generated electricity and distributed it to some 400 lamps lit by his incandescent bulb. By the turn of the century, 20 million such lamps would glow.

Edison, hailed as "the Wizard of Menlo Park," was the most prolific of the inventors transforming the way Americans lived. He and his team obtained no fewer than 1,093 patents, including the motion picture camera and projector. In garages across America, other inventors were working on the internal combustion engine, which would create a wholly unexpected new market for the petroleum that flowed through Rockefeller's refineries. This was the entrepreneurial essence of American inventive genius: New products not only rendered daily life easier but also generated new industries to employ workers who then could afford to buy the products.

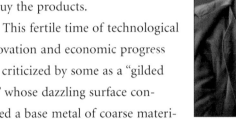

This fertile time of technological innovation and economic progress was criticized by some as a "gilded age" whose dazzling surface concealed a base metal of coarse materialism. To be sure, the all-consuming passion of Americans seemed to be the pursuit of money. Newspaper pundit Finley Peter Dunne, from whose pen dripped the brogue-ish wisdom of Mr. Dooley, observed that the "crownin' wurruk iv our civilization is th' cash raygister."

The phrase "gilded age" came from the title of a satirical novel co-authored by Mark Twain *(inset)*. *The Gilded Age* was published in 1873, three years before Twain's first great success, *The Adventures of Tom Sawyer.* Although Twain would be remembered for Tom Sawyer, Huck Finn, and other characters rooted in his boyhood experiences in the Mississippi River town of Hannibal, Missouri, he was known then for his biting social satire. He delighted in ridiculing the get-rich mania of his countrymen even as he pursued one risky scheme after another, hoping to increase his own considerable literary profits.

Until her death in 1883, Sojourner Truth fought for black equality and women's suffrage. Born a slave, she took her new name as a preacher of the truth who would not remain in any one place.

Clara Barton, founder of the American Red Cross in 1881 and a symbol of charitable self-sacrifice, began her career as a volunteer caring for Union soldiers on the battlefields of the Civil War.

What concerned many critics was the increasing concentration of wealth in the hands of titans they called "robber barons." Unquestionably ruthless as well as resourceful, these entrepreneurs frequently operated at the edge of ethics and the law. "What do I care about law?" asked the railroad tycoon Cornelius Vanderbilt. "Hain't I got the power?" But their relentless drive also helped propel economic progress. Rockefeller in particular gave back much of what he took. His contributions to education and other good works would exceed half a billion dollars.

Millions of Americans admired the industrialists for their success as much as for their philanthropy. Some even tried to rationalize the conduct and prosperity of big business by applying Darwin's theory of biological evolution to the economic sphere. According to a notion known as Social Darwinism, the struggle for profits rewarded the strong and eliminated the weak. "The growth of a large business is merely the survival of the fittest," Rockefeller himself told his Baptist Sunday school class. "It is merely the working out of a law of nature and a law of God."

Ideas about biological adaptation also helped dictate the role of women. Evolution, it was said, had determined that female members of the human species should be wives, mothers, housekeepers, teachers, nurses, and secretaries and should not bother themselves with male occupations—or preoccupations such as voting. Only in Wyoming Territory could women cast the ballot, a right first exercised in 1870. The idea of community property in a marriage was a chimera that crossed the minds of only the most radical feminists. Until 1882, the husband legally owned even the clothing and jewelry he had given his wife.

Even Clara Barton, the founder of the American Red Cross and one of the few women able to break through the barriers to high achievement, followed the accepted path for much of her life. She was a teacher, a clerk in the U.S. Patent Office, and then a freelance caregiver during the Civil War. What stamped Barton as special was her single-minded determination in nursing wounded soldiers and distributing medical supplies on the battlefields even though she lacked official affiliation. In 1881, Barton organized the first American branch of the International Red Cross. She personally led humanitarian relief expeditions at natural disasters such as the Johnstown flood in 1889 *(page 35)*. And at the age of 76, she landed on the beach of Cuba to supervise the care of casualties during the Spanish-American War.

Another remarkable woman, Sojourner Truth, embodied the struggle for equal rights for African Americans as well as for women. She was born Isabella Baumfree, a slave, in upstate New York. Set free in 1827, she worked as a domestic and began preaching on street corners in New York City. Unable to read or write but six feet tall and blessed with a deep voice and a thick Dutch accent picked up from her original owner, she exuded powerful personal magnetism and often electrified audiences with her brash style: Once, faced with an audience of men who challenged her womanhood, she dared to bare her breasts.

Taking her new name, she later went on the road with little more than 25 cents and a bag of clothing to proclaim the causes of blacks and women, but both were losing momentum by the time of her death in 1883. The women's suffrage movement failed to win the constitutional amendment it sought, and black gains symbolized by the election of Hiram Revels soon faded. After 1890, African Americans could not even vote in Southern states, which invoked poll taxes, literacy tests, and property qualifications to disenfranchise them. At the same time, new Jim Crow laws brought racial segregation to virtually every aspect of public life in the South—and few Northerners objected. In 1896, the U.S. Supreme Court ruled in *Plessy v. Ferguson* that "separate but equal" accommodations in everything from railroad cars to public schools were lawful under the Constitution.

The revival of bigotry that held down African Americans, however, could not stem the tide of religious and ethnic diversity spilling upon U.S. shores. More than 12 million immigrants reached America during the final

In 1882, the copper head and torch of the Statue of Liberty await assembly atop her torso in Paris. A gift of the French people, the 151-foot-tall Lady Liberty had to be taken apart before shipment to New York, where she welcomed immigrants to America.

three decades of the century. After the dedication of the Statue of Liberty in 1886, those arriving in New York were welcomed by the words of the poet Emma Lazarus inscribed upon the pedestal of Lady Liberty: "Give me your tired, your poor, your huddled masses yearning to breathe free." Increasingly, immigrants were the tired and poor of central and southern Europe, and they flocked to large eastern industrial centers already bulging with emigrants from rural America.

While immigrants poured in, the continent's original inhabitants were being penned up on reservations. As recently as the Civil War, perhaps 250,000 Native Americans had still roamed the Rocky Mountains and the Great Plains. As miners, cattlemen, and settlers intruded upon their ancestral lands, the Sioux, Blackfoot, Comanche, Apache, and other tribes fought back. "We took away their country and their means of support," wrote General Philip Sheridan, "broke up their mode of living, their habits of life, introduced disease and decay among them, and it was for this and against this that they made war. Could anyone expect less?"

The Indian wars endured for 25 years, pitting tribesman against soldier in hundreds of battles. But the Indians were defeated not so much by the army as by the slaughter of the buffalo, which they depended on for food, fuel, clothing, and other essentials. Most moved to the reservation—but not Geronimo (inset) and his Chiricahua Apaches. In 1876,

he fled the barren San Carlos reservation in Arizona and resumed his people's defense of their homeland. Geronimo surrendered in 1883 but escaped again. In 1886, when he surrendered for the last time to the soldiers he called white eyes, it marked the end of a melancholy chapter in the history of the Western frontier.

By the 1890s, that frontier no longer existed. The historian Frederick Jackson Turner, writing in 1893, proclaimed the Western frontier closed. He believed that the frontier experience, which successively had affected every section of the country, had done much to shape American life. To it he attributed the rugged individualism of Americans and the democratic character of their society. "For nearly 300 years the dominant fact in American life has been expansion," he wrote. "That these energies of expansion will no longer operate would be a rash prediction."

Soon these "energies of expansion" sought frontiers beyond the North American continent. Although the United States had long isolated itself from world affairs—"an apart nation," as President Benjamin Henry Harrison characterized it in 1888—economic considerations stimulated interest in international affairs. Industrialists needed new markets to keep their factories running. Moreover, the notion that it was the nation's manifest destiny to settle the West was now extended to the entire world. Many thought it America's duty to bring not only manufactured goods but also Christianity and the blessings of democracy to other peoples. As early as 1867, the same year the United States purchased Alaska from Russia, the nation took over

The legendary Chiricahua Apache chief Geronimo poses defiantly with his rifle a year after his final surrender to U.S. Army forces in 1886.

A body lies amid the furniture, barrels, and remains of houses littering Johnstown, Pennsylvania, after river waters ravaged the city in 1889. The flood claimed some 2,200 lives.

Riding high in the saddle in Cuba, Colonel Theodore Roosevelt commands his Rough Riders, the regiment of cowboy and blueblood volunteers he raised to fight the Spaniards in 1898.

the Midway Islands far out in the Pacific. In 1887, the re-vitalized navy established a base at Pearl Harbor. Six years later, marines helped local white businessmen overthrow the government of Hawaii, which soon would be annexed by the United States.

But America's dramatic debut on the world stage came in 1898. Not far from Florida, on the island of Cuba, Spain was engaged in a brutal suppression of a local insurrection. American sympathy for the underdog Cubans was heightened by sensational reports of Spanish atrocities appearing in New York newspapers *(pages 122-129).* "You furnish the pictures," William Randolph Hearst, publisher of *The New York Journal,* wired an artist he had dispatched to Cuba, "and I'll furnish the war." When the battleship *Maine,* sent there to show the flag, blew up in Havana harbor, killing 266 crewmen, the newspapers blamed the Spaniards. Although spontaneous combustion in one of the ship's powder magazines proba-bly set off the explosion, the United States soon declared war on Spain.

The Spanish-American War lasted only four months but brought to the fore a hero of enduring reputation. Theodore Roosevelt was an advocate of the rugged life, a once-sickly child who had learned to box, ride, and shoot to strengthen himself. As assistant secretary of the navy, he sent the ships that destroyed the Spanish fleet in the Philippines and set the stage for U.S. occupation of that Pacific outpost. He then resigned in order to organize the First U.S. Volunteer Cavalry Regiment—a group of cow-boys, ranchers, and Ivy League bluebloods known as the Rough Riders *(left).* Landing in Cuba as part of a 17,000-man expeditionary force, Colonel Roosevelt led the Rough Riders in a storied assault up San Juan Hill near Santiago.

Thanks to this "splendid little war," as the diplomat John Hay described it, Cuba became a virtual American protectorate and the United States gained Puerto Rico, Guam, the Philippines—and a charismatic new leader. Three years later, Teddy Roosevelt would become presi-dent and lead America to prominence in the new century.

The Frontier

★

AN EXPANDING AMERICA

A tent city sprawls across the prairie at Guthrie, Indian Territory, only five days after the opening of the Oklahoma region to white settlers. On April 22, 1889, the first day, 15,000 people from 32 states swarmed in to stake claims. By the end of the first week Guthrie had 50 saloons.

The Promised Land

War whoops of Indians attacking settlers. The crack of Winchesters as the cavalry canters to the rescue. Shootouts in Dodge City. Masked cowpunchers clubbing sheep to death. Custer's yellow mane fluttering as he awaits the oncoming Sioux at Little Big Horn. Gunfight at the OK Corral. Calamity Jane, Bat Masterson, Billy the Kid, Buffalo Bill, Wyatt Earp, Wild Bill Hickok. Nothing else in the entire American pageant matched the sweep and excitement of the Wild West. Yet all this flamboyance tended to obscure the central fact that the real frontier story was the story of plain people struggling for land.

During the Civil War, the trans-Mississippi Great Plains were opened up by the Union government to free homesteading. An act of Congress gave 160 acres of land to anyone willing to work it—making an egalitarian dream come true. In England, the workers crammed into their slums put the dream to song: "To the west, to the west, to the land of the free, / Where mighty Missouri rolls down to the sea; / Where a man is a man if he's willing to toil; / And the humblest may gather the fruits of the soil; / Where the young may exult and the aged may rest; / Away, far away, to the land of the west."

The West offered a chance for a new start, and between 1870 and 1890 the greatest migration in American history increased the population of the trans-Mississippi west from fewer than seven million to more than 16 million. They were all kinds: boys in blue who had dreamed around wartime campfires of homesteading on the prairies; boys in gray who had fled the South's postwar anarchy to start anew; scoundrels seeking a fast buck; Mennonite immigrants smuggling the fabulous Turkey Red wheat out of the Crimea into the Dakotas; native-born Americans quitting overcrowded, worn-out family farms for "oceans of land, ready for the plow, good as the best in America, yet lying without occupants."

Jouncing west in her covered wagon, Jane Grout wrote in her diary: "Farther we go, better I like it." But for most emigrants, the farther west they went, the closer they came to the reality of the frontier. The land of opportunity was also one of plagues, drought, storms, epidemics, and fierce extremes of heat and cold. And along with the struggle to stay alive, another more visible battle was shaping up with land speculators, cattlemen and Indians.

The Great Plains so coveted by the newcomers belonged for the most part to the Indians. Successively dispossessed and pushed westward, they

"Thoughts stray back to the comfortable homes we left behind and the question arises, is this a good move? The wagon train is divided, some want to turn back; others favor going on. A decision is reached at noon; the train is to move on."

Diary of Mrs. Lucy A. Ide, 1878

Homesteaders rest by their covered wagons in Colorado in the 1870s. The trip from Ohio or Indiana—1,100 miles—took about two months.

George Custer, vain and headstrong, wore his blond hair to his shoulders and always carried a toothbrush—even in the field—to polish his gleaming teeth after every meal.

The great Lakota chief Sitting Bull, killed in 1890 when police composed of members of his own tribe attempted to arrest him, was reported to have said late in his life, "I am the last Indian."

had been solemnly deeded most of the Great Plains by 1840, a time when the region was universally and inaccurately called the Great American Desert. It would take another third of a century, 928 officially recorded clashes, and a series of blatant betrayals at the hands of white America to force the Indians from their "desert."

The Sioux uprising of 1876 epitomized the process. One of the trans-Mississippi areas that the Sioux had received in perpetuity was the Dakota Black Hills, a region so forbidding that Washington thought the settlers never would covet it. But early in the 1870s came rumors that there was gold in the hills. Once more, pressured by land seekers, Washington asked the Sioux to move. When the Indians refused, the government announced that whites could enter the Black Hills at their own risk.

Predictably, 15,000 fortune seekers invaded the Sioux territory, and just as predictably the Sioux rose under Chiefs Crazy Horse and Sitting Bull. They annihilated a cavalry force of 246, incautiously led by the glory-hunting General George Custer. Then, four months later, tired of running, the Indian war party surrendered. Bayoneted in captivity, the dying Crazy Horse called to the soldier who had wounded him: "Let me go, my friend, you have hurt me enough." Sitting Bull, who had fled to Canada, returned in 1881, and several years later, while being put under precautionary arrest, was also killed.

The Indians were defeated, but the conflict over the western lands had just begun. From the moment it became apparent that the Great Plains was not a desert but a treasure, all manner of Americans began to fight over the prize. The railroads grabbed the largest share—181 million acres of land, six times the size of Pennsylvania—for building half a dozen rail links with the West *(page 59),* and consequently they became the largest landholders in the country.

The cattlemen, in their usual style, simply took for grazing huge chunks of public domain, generally an average of 30 to 40 square miles apiece, and waved off with cocked guns newcomers who questioned their title. Land speculators built holdings of up to 600,000 acres apiece, using a bagful of tricks: They falsified dates of occupancy, stole choice sites from settlers by legal chicanery, and filed for free homesteads in different states under different names. Overall, half a billion acres of U.S. land went to major land-holders and only 80 million to homesteaders; despite the national commitment to give free land to the masses, probably only one acre in nine was thus apportioned.

The real rulers of the prairie were the cattle ranchers. Raising their low-cost livestock on free land that was so rich in grass that, according to one rancher, it could "make the dollars crawl right into yer jeans," the cattlemen dominated the West until 1885. Then in the mid-1880s, the undisciplined cattlemen overreached themselves. Rocketing prices brought overproduction; prices dropped 40 percent. A summer of drought and one of the worst winters in history completed the rout; spring revealed that nearly 90 percent of the animals on the range were dead. Hundreds of ranch owners pulled out (among them Theodore Roosevelt, who turned over his Dakota holdings to his hands and took the train back East). The cattleman's hegemony over the prairie was broken; from now on western lands would belong to those who had been promised them in the first place—the homesteading farmers.

Unlike the cattlemen in their bonanza years, the sodbusters who came west in their wagons found no natural compatibility with their environment, but had to tame it—or bend to it—from the start. To a newcomer who said, "This would be a fine country if we just had water," an old-timer snorted, "Yes, so would hell."

At times even hell might have seemed more comfortable. The family's first shelter was usually a sod-faced dugout cut into a hillside, so small, said one settler, that "we had to put the bed outside in the daytime and the table at night." Cornmeal, salt pork, and sorghum were the food staples. Cut-down gunnysacks became men's pants, and calico, bought during rare visits to town, was made up into a year's wardrobe of two dresses. Snakes, mice, and bedbugs flourished in the sod house (pages 46-47); so did disease. Cholera, smallpox, typhoid fever, and diphtheria came in epidemics, and malaria was so common that sufferers said, "That's nothing, we only have the ager."

Frontier life was hardest of all for prairie women (pages 54-55). Childbirth was a dread; the doctors were far away, usually ill-trained and quite often drunkards. The first law passed in the Dakotas relating to doctors was a statute specifying that a physician must be tried for manslaughter if he poisoned a patient while intoxicated.

Every day brought a grinding succession of the most

Russian peasants such as these in the Dakota Territory generally settled in the northern reaches, which resembled their native steppes.

Blackfoot women and children sit in front of their tepee in the Montana
Territory in 1881. By then almost all the fighting bands had been pushed
onto reservations, and the end of the nomadic Indian civilization was near.
"When we sit down, we grow pale and die," mourned a Kiowa chief.

primitive chores—making soap and candles, drawing water, feeding livestock, struggling to keep a dirt house clean,
or spending half a day softening the harsh alkali water to
wash the family clothes. But it was simple loneliness that
seemed hardest to bear. The endless, monotonous space
and the silence broken only by the constant keening of the
wind, drove some to depression and occasionally to mad-
ness. One farm woman, discovering a dandelion growing,
carefully cultivated it and saved the seeds, explaining, "I felt
less lonely." Another isolated settler, Mrs. James McClure,
heard that another woman had come to live miles away.

Taking her two small children, she walked across the
prairie until she reached the other's cabin. The women
stood looking at each other and then—utter strangers—
threw their arms around each other and wept and laughed.

There was, in addition, constant danger from
plagues, blizzards, prairie fires, tornadoes and, at first, Indians. In 1874 grasshoppers swarmed across the central
plains, hiding the sun, devouring the greenery, mosquito
netting, clothes, even plow handles, and leaving, said one
farmer, "nothing but the mortgage." On another day in
January 1888, the School Children's Storm swooped

A pioneer family poses in front of its sod house on the Kansas prairie. The sods for such dwellings were turned up in long strips by steel plows, then chopped into short sections and laid atop each other like bricks, making an insulated house that was warm in winter and cool in summer.

down while the children were still in school or starting home, freezing to death more than 200 youngsters.

Some families quit and stormed back east, their wagons bearing such signs as "In God we trusted, in Kansas we busted." Most settlers stayed, however, and between 1870 and 1900 they tamed 430 million acres of tough land, in the process all but eliminating the American buffalo, the hides of which had become valuable commodities. By 1890 the report of the Census Bureau announced a historic change: "There can hardly be said to be a frontier line."

Though the physical frontier had all but vanished,

"My husband, I pity he is wasting his life / To obtain a scant living for his children and wife. / The Sabbath which once was a day of sweet rest / Is now spent toiling for bread in the west. / After five years hard toiling with hopes that were in vain / I have such despair on this desolate plain."
—Song by Mrs. A. M. Green, Greeley, Colorado, 1887

A trader sits atop a mountain of buffalo hides near Dodge City, Kansas, 1874. In 1872, during its first three months of existence, Dodge City shipped east 43,029 buffalo hides and 1.4 million pounds of buffalo meat.

the frontiersman's hunger for land had not. There was still one piece of Indian land left in an area soon to be called Oklahoma, the last of the old-time permanent Indian territory assigned by the federal government and still held by 22 tribes. Now, once more, the land seekers besieged Washington. Once more the Indians were told to move aside. At noon, April 22, 1889, pistol shots opened 1.92 million acres to 100,000 eager men lined up and waiting on the border—on foot, on horse, in carts and in 15 overflowing Santa Fe trains. By that night, Guthrie and Oklahoma City were established, every last acre had been claimed, and men sat with guns and guarded their land.

Perhaps the most disgraceful episode in the history of America's unconscionable treatment of its native population took place in 1890, when the U.S. Cavalry massacred a group of Indians who had been taken into custody and were encamped at Wounded Knee, South Dakota. In the process of taking away the few weapons the band of Indians still possessed the soldiers mistook the actions of a deaf Indian as hostile and opened fire with deadly breech-loading Hotchkiss guns; by the time the shooting stopped, 250 Lakota men, women, and children lay dead. The frontier had finally been conquered. But at what cost?

Chief Big Foot lies dead in the snow, a victim of the U.S. Cavalry at Wounded Knee, South Dakota, in 1890.

Nineteen days after Wounded Knee, General Nelson Miles and
his staff inspect the vanquished tribe. On this day, January 16,
1891, the Sioux surrendered, ending America's Indian wars.

"Hoo-oo! My children, my children. In days behind I called you to travel the
hunting trail or to follow the war trail. Now those trails are choked with sand;
they are covered with grass; the young men cannot find them. Today I call upon
you to travel a new trail, the only trail now open—the White Man's Road."
—Wovoka, Paiute Chief, 1891

Prospectors camp in the Colorado Rockies. "I do not see," said one miner, "how any young man can content himself working for wages."

"1,000 lbs. flour, 400 lbs. bacon, 4 gallons vinegar, 200 lbs. sugar, 150 lbs. beans, 2 gallons pickles, 100 lbs. dried beef, 50 lbs. salt, 2 doz. boxes of matches, 50 lbs. dried fruit, 1 coffee mill, 30 lbs. rice, 25 lbs. soap, 3 camp kettles, 10 lbs. pepper, 8 lbs. tea, 50 lbs. lead for bullets, 6 lbs. cream tarter, 3 lbs. soda, 1,000 gun caps."

–Six months' provisions for four prospectors

Surveyors pause before descending a bluff near Silverton, Colorado.
"If anyone thinks it is fun, let him try it, that's all," wrote a surveyor.

Dakota farm women take a rare break from their chores to get together in a neighbor's house and exchange gossip at a quilting bee.

An Overland stage heads out from its station at Calvin, Montana. The six-horse teams covered the 10 miles between regular stations in about an hour; then fresh teams were harnessed up. Every fourth or fifth stop was a home station, where passengers could get grub, whiskey, and a bed.

"*The best seat in a stage is the one next to the driver. If the team runs away—sit still and take your chances. If you jump, nine out of ten times you will get hurt. Don't smoke a strong pipe inside the coach—spit on the leeward side. Don't lop over neighbors when sleeping. Never shoot on the road as the noise might frighten the horses. Don't discuss politics or religion. Don't grease your hair, because travel is dusty.*"

–Tips for stage riders, *Omaha Herald*, 1877

Eastern sportsmen and their wives, hunting from their private rail car, City of Worcester, pause during a safari into the Great Plains.

A rail crew building the Northern Pacific link between Washington Territory and Minnesota poses on a mountain trestle in 1885.

"In the early days of the first Pacific Railroad, and before the herds had been driven back from the tracks, singular hunting parties were sometimes seen on the buffalo range. These hunters were capitalists connected with the newly-constructed roads; and some of them now for the first time bestrode a horse, while few had ever used firearms. These were amusing excursions where a merry party of pleasant officers from a frontier post, and their guests, a jolly crowd of merchants, brokers, and railroad men from the East start out to have a buffalo hunt. With them go the post guide and a scout or two, the escort of soldiers, and the great blue army wagons, under whose white tilts are piled all the comforts that the post can furnish—unlimited food and drink, and many sacks of forage for the animals. Here all was mirth and jest and good fellowship, and the hunters lived in as much comfort as when at home. The killing of the buffalo was to them an excuse for their jolly outing amidst novel scenes."

–*Scribner's* magazine, September 1892

Against snow-shrouded Old Baldie in the northern Rockies, children and their teacher play Ring-a-Rosie in their schoolyard. Pioneer settlers gave high priority to educating youngsters; only a few days after a new settlement had been established, the men would join to build a schoolhouse.

Frontier Justice

"I never killed nary a feller what didn't need it."

New Mexico marshal Clay Allison

Lynched by the angry burghers of Minneapolis in 1882, rapist Frank McManus swings from a tree limb after being dragged from jail.

Not far beneath the prim, lace-curtained surface of Victorian America lay a deep and abiding potential for violence. In 1870, only five years after the Civil War and the assassination of President Lincoln, the odor of blood still lingered across the land. In the big cities of the East, as thousands of penniless European immigrants poured into the urban ghettos, the efforts of local police forces to keep order collapsed under the impact of sheer numbers. By 1870 gangs of young toughs were ravaging the poorer areas of most big cities almost at will. In the last decade of the century, a new criminal phenomenon appeared on the scene: an internationally controlled underground of organized racketeering. In 1890 the nation was appalled to learn that New Orleans' police chief, David Hennessy, had been assassinated by a secret criminal group from Sicily called the Mafia Fifteen. Mafia leaders were captured and tried, but the intimidated jury failed to convict a single one. Incensed at this obvious dereliction of duty, a group of New Orleans' most zealous citizens formed a posse, stormed the jailhouse, and shot, clubbed, or hanged 11 of the Sicilians. Given this failure of public enforcement authorities to deal with escalating crime, it is little wonder that the nation's most effective crime-fighting operation was a private outfit, the Pinkerton Detective Agency *(page 72)*.

In the West, the situation was even worse. Bands of outlaws terrorized the border states, in defiance of police and militia; many of the badmen, like two brothers named Frank and Jesse James *(page 70)*, were discharged Confederate soldiers. In the mining camps and cattle towns of the western frontier, the deeds of gunslingers, claim jumpers, and cattle rustlers were accepted conditions of life, a situation which forced shipping companies such as Wells Fargo *(page 65)* to go to extraordinary lengths to protect their precious cargo. And while many western sheriffs worked hard and honestly to keep the peace, many other purported representatives of law and order were simply quick-triggered hoodlums. Sheriff Wyatt Earp, himself a saloon bouncer, deputized a card sharp called Bat Masterson to help him clean up Dodge City, Kansas, and later drafted an alcoholic murderer named Doc Holliday to pacify Tombstone, Arizona. Wild Bill Hickok, the high-rolling marshal of Abilene, Kansas, calmly boasted that he was responsible for "considerably over a hundred" deaths, several of them rumored to be outside the line of duty; and no one believed frontier marshal Clay Allison when he denied that he killed for pleasure.

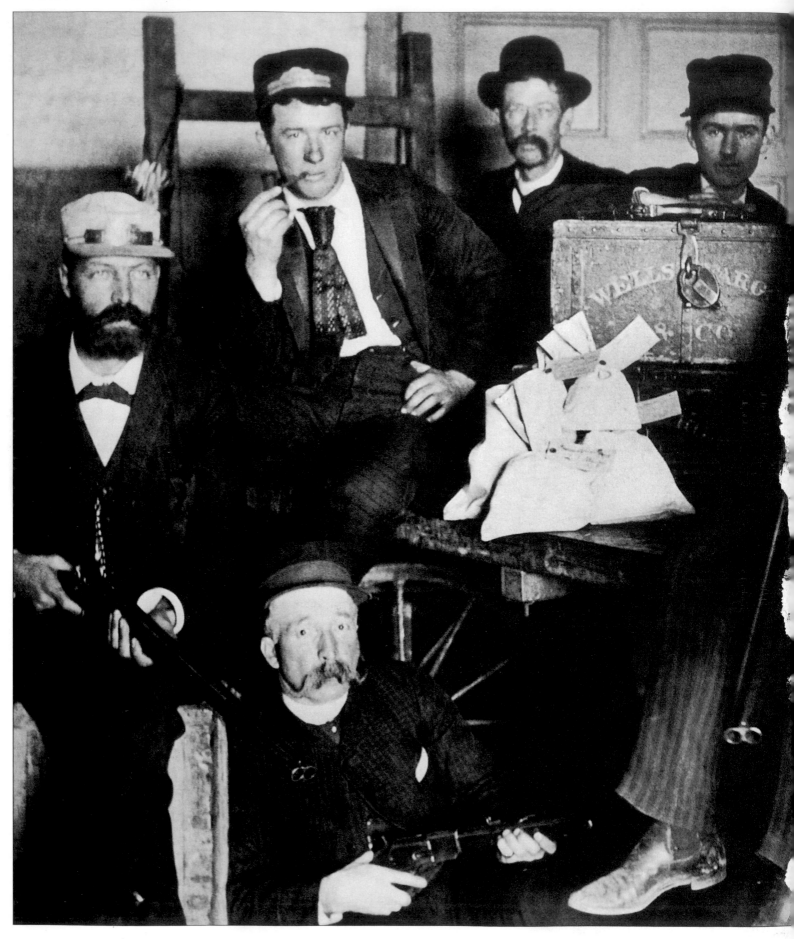

An intrepid squad of agents keeps watch over bags and strongboxes full of Nevada silver at the Wells Fargo branch office in Reno.

"Alert and Faithful"

Guards ride shotgun on a Wells Fargo shipment worth $350,000.

One of the staunchest defenders of law and order on the western frontier was an express agency called Wells Fargo, the trans-Mississippi arm of the American Express Company. Set up in 1852 initially to speed gold shipments from the California minefields to the banks and minting offices back east, Wells Fargo had expanded by 1870 into a network of 396 branch offices, stagecoach routes, and railway express franchises that reached into virtually every cowtown and mining camp in the West.

For a fee, the company would carry just about anything: mail, bank notes, brides en route from the East to booming California, and on at least one occasion, a battalion of soldiers to fight an Indian war. The backbone of the firm's trade, however, was the gold and silver that it transported in the padlocked green strongboxes that became a Wells Fargo trademark.

Tempted by such rich prizes, bands of outlaws hovered around the Wells Fargo routes like flies around honey. But true to its motto—"Alert and Faithful"—the company hired gun-toting guards to fend off these marauders. And to track down any outlaws who might grab the gold and get away, in 1873 Wells Fargo hired a California sheriff named James B. Hume, who steadfastly pursued Wells Fargo robbers for the next 31 years. A burly six-footer, Hume was a maverick among the West's gunslinging lawmen. His favorite diversions were tending his rose garden and savoring fine claret and imported French cheese. To the tough business of frontier crime detection, he added such refinements of science as ballistics and his own annotated photographic rogue's gallery *(right)*. So successful were his methods that he was able to report after a 14-year period that only $415,312.55 out of the hundreds of millions of dollars' worth of treasure shipped by Wells Fargo had been lost to outlaws. And of this, Wells Fargo customers lost not a penny. For it was a bedrock company policy to guarantee that every cent lost would instantly be refunded.

MR. JNO. J. VALENTINE
Wells, Fargo & Company,
San Francisco,

Dear Sir:

We have compiled from the records in our Department the following data, extending over a period of fourteen years—from November 5th, 1870, to November 5th, 1884.

Total amount taken from W. F. & Co.'s Express by stage robbers, train robbers and burglars during the fourteen years beginning November 5, 1870.	*$415,312.55*
Rewards paid for arrest and conviction of said robbers, etc., and percentage paid on treasure recovered	*$73,451.00*
Number of Stage Robberies and Attempted Stage Robberies	*347*
Number of Burglaries	*23*
Number of Train Robberies and Attempted Train Robberies	*8*
Number of Convictions for Robbery and Attempt at Stage Robbery	*206*
Number of Convictions for Train Robbery and attempt at same	*20*
Number of Convictions for Burglary	*14*
Number of W. F. & Co.'s Guards killed while in discharge of duty, by stage robbers	*2*
Number of Stage Drivers killed by robbers	*4*
Number of Passengers killed by stage robbers	*4*
Number of Stage Robbers killed while in the act of robbery or attempting to rob the express on stages, by W. F. & Co's guard	*5*
Number of Robbers killed while resisting arrest	*11*
Number of Robbers hanged by citizens	*7*

You will notice by the foregoing that the number of lives lost, as the result of the above enumerated robberies and attempted robberies, amounts to THIRTY-THREE.

There have also been seven horses killed, and thirteen stolen from the various stage teams.

Respectfully submitted,
J.B. Hume, J.N. Thacker, Special Officers

Frank Miller

Robbed Stage Six miles above Ukiah. Jany 15th 1896 Sent to State Prison for a term of 15 years.

Jesus Marea

Robbed three Stages in 1875 Butte Co. with Pardilla, "Red Antone" and others

.:Hugh, Mc Gregor :.

.:A Crank :.

Wᵐ Corbet - Stage Robber.

John D. Ruggles.
In an attempt to rob the Weaver-
-ville Stage murdered W. F. & Cos
Mess. Buck Montgomery. May 14-92
Taken from prison and hanged by the mob
July 24. 1892.

Eugene Tyler
(Negro) Robbed Los Baños
Stage May 7-1877 with
Dan Mc Carty

J. R. Todd
Robbed stage near Glendale Or
alone July 25/83

Geo Harris
Attempted to rob Stage
from Yreka to Redding
alone June 26" 1882

Geo W. Rugg
Robbed Marysville Stage
July 31-1877 with
Eph White

John McCabe
Burglarized R.R.& Ex.
Safe Madison. Yolo Co.
June 14-84

Tom Horn
Letter Thief

John A. Toney
Robbed Shasta Stage three
times in one week in 1876
with Frank Chapman

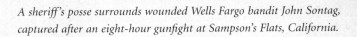

Vigilante Vengeance

In many parts of the wide-open West, the law was nothing more than an angry citizen with a gun or a rope. Sometimes these citizens banded together into vigilante committees, such as the ones that first warned *(inset)* and then shot or hanged misbehavers in the Montana Territory. In other cases, outraged individuals just grabbed their six-shooters and started firing.

One memorable instance occurred during 1876 in Northfield, Minnesota, when the swift trigger fingers of local citizens broke up the most notorious outlaw gang in all the West. It began quietly enough. At midmorning on September 7, 1876, five tall, handsome strangers trotted into

Northfield, mounted on fine horses with fancy saddles. "Nobler looking fellows I never saw," exclaimed one witness later. The strangers idled about town until two in the afternoon, when they rode up to the bank. At that moment, two additional strangers came galloping onto the main street, yelling and firing off their revolvers in an attempt to frighten people into taking cover. "Them men are going for the town, they mean to rob the bank!" a bystander shouted.

And indeed they did. The invaders grabbed all the cash they could find, which turned out to be only $12 in loose scrip, fatally shot cashier Joseph Heywood, and ran outside—to find not a deserted street but a crowd of gunslinging citizens. Henry M. Wheeler, a medical student home in Northfield for the summer, picked off one horseman, a man named Clell Miller. Another robber, Bill Chadwell, was cut down by hardware merchant A.R. Manning. The other desperadoes rapidly fled town.

During the next two weeks, while posses hunted the robbers, state police authorities speculated that the gang leaders were none other than Jesse James and the Younger brothers. The outlaw band they headed had already knocked over 10 other banks, pillaged four trains and two stage coaches, snatched the gate receipts of the Kansas City Fair, and gunned down 15 people.

Acting on a tip from a youth named August Suborn, a posse under Sheriff James Glispin ran the fugitives to earth on September 21, some 80 miles southwest of Northfield. A second gun battle erupted, and when the smoke had cleared, the posse had killed one more desperado, Charlie Pitts, and captured three others—who turned out to be the nefarious Younger brothers. Jesse James had split off from the gang earlier and remained at large.

Hurting from many bullet wounds and in mortal fear of being lynched, the three Youngers were carted back to jail. To their surprise, they were treated like celebrities. The good Minnesota farmers felt a grudging admiration for the bandits, and they flocked to the jailhouse to see what the men looked like. Photographers took pictures of the gang members, both living and dead, and sold over 50,000 souvenir prints—some with misspelled names *(right)*—in a single month. Awaiting trial, the brothers shrewdly played up to their public by sweet-talking visitors, displaying just the right note of contrition ("We were drove to it, sir," Cole Younger declared; "circumstances sometimes makes men what they are.") and graciously accepting the gifts of food, cigars, and flowers brought by admiring ladies. Amid this aura of good will the Youngers beat the hangman and got off with life sentences. As for Jesse James, he went on robbing and killing for another six years, until he was shot in the head by a member of his own gang, Bob Ford, in 1882, for $10,000 in reward money.

A Northfield souvenir card (right) showed the good guys at top and the bad guys below. The photographs of Chadwell, Miller, and Pitts are posthumous.

August Suborn, Surveyor

Haywood, Cashier

Glispin, Sheriff

Cole Younger

Chadwell & Miller

Bob Younger

Jim Younger

Charly Pitts

Jacoby Photo
Minneapolis

The Pioneering Private Eye

In the free enterprise spirit of the nineteenth century, the most powerful U.S. organization for catching crooks was neither the federal government nor the local police, but a private detective company run by a Scottish immigrant named Allan Pinkerton. In the best Horatio Alger style, Pinkerton had come off the boat from Glasgow in 1842 a penniless young man, and before 1900 his National Detective Agency had become a million-dollar empire whose activities were worldwide. The son of a Glasgow police sergeant, Pinkerton had been forced to flee Scotland at age 23 to avoid arrest for taking part in political riots. En route to America, his sailing packet was wrecked on an island off Nova Scotia. After reaching shore in a lifeboat, Pinkerton eventually made his way to the Chicago area with total assets of one silver dollar tied up in a handkerchief.

After assisting the local sheriff to track down a gang of counterfeiters, Pinkerton decided the crime-busting business was for him. Appointed a deputy sheriff, he acquired such a reputation at running in malefactors that Chicago's chief law officer hired him as an investigator. Two years later he struck out on his own as a private detective. Lining up clients among the city's railroads, he put together a 10-man organization he called Pinkerton's National Detective Agency. To dramatize its promised vigilance in pursuit of criminals, he later took for his trademark an unsleeping, all-seeing eye *(inset)*. By 1870 his agency included thousands of highly trained agents.

By the early 1880s, however, the elder Pinkerton, ailing and bored with the increasing administrative burden of running his empire, turned over much of the operation to his deputies. He never lost his joy in the hunt, and he continued to chase criminals in the field until his death in 1884, from gangrene that developed after he had tripped and bitten his tongue during his customary morning constitutional.

The will of the once penniless immigrant left an estate of half a million dollars; William and another son, Robert, inherited control of the agency. In 1897 William was handed a report on a band of outlaws that was pillaging Union Pacific trains. The gang was composed, the report said, "of outlaws and former cowboys, headed by George LeRoy Parker, alias Butch Cassidy, a cowboy, rustler, and gambler." Cassidy, a likable bandit with an infectious smile and twinkling eyes, had left his father's Utah ranch in the late 1880s to follow the outlaw trail simply for the glamor of it. And a glamorous time he had, pulling together a swashbuckling crew known as the Wild Bunch *(left)*.

To stop them William Pinkerton sent out the renowned cowboy detective Charlie Siringo. Posing as a Texas gunslinger, Siringo joined the Bunch and tipped off the railroad whenever a heist was planned. As Siringo's cover wore thin, forcing him to quit the gang, the railroad adopted other tactics—a pioneer type of mobile striking force *(right)*. So successful were these tactics in frustrating the train robbers that Cassidy and company were forced to lay off the U. P. for easier game—like other railroads.

We never sleep.

Celebrating after a heist, the Wild Bunch sits for a portrait.

To foil the Wild Bunch, the Union Pacific outfitted a high-speed train with horse stalls and this posse of determined manhunters.

Holidays

COMMUNAL OCCASIONS FOR FUN

High-schoolers prepare to decorate veterans' graves.

Decoration Day,
May 30, 1899

Illustrated calendar

"I have been out paying New Year's calls since twelve o'clock. A tiresome, hollow sham it is, but I must keep it up until near midnight."

Godey's Lady's Book, January 1870

"The Luxury of Guilt"

In an era of hard work, rural isolation, and monumental inhibition, holidays were liberating occasions. Easter parades offered a socially acceptable chance to show off; Valentine's Day afforded an opportunity for shy maidens to send ornate tokens of affection to their beaux. On the warm-weather holidays, frontier farmers who had endured the frozen isolation of the winter prairie came to town to crack open a convivial keg or two, and to find out—often for the first time in months—what had been happening to their neighbors and to their nation. So strongly felt was the need for this kind of lusty communalizing that many U.S. holidays got their start as national institutions in the decade just after the Civil War.

One such occasion was Arbor Day, launched April 22, 1875, by J. Sterling Morton of Nebraska as part of a campaign to get people to plant trees on the bare prairie. Within a dozen years, 40 states had named April 22 an official holiday, and 600 million newly planted trees adorned the nation's plains. Another of the new observances was Memorial Day, whose date was designated as May 30 by John A. Logan of the Grand Army of the Republic (but as April 26 by an unreconstructed band of Mississippi ladies) to honor the Civil War dead. The scene on Memorial Day was much the same in thousands of small towns across the United States. Typically the day began with a parade led by a brass band and the volunteer firemen hand-pulling their pumping engine. Following them were the Mexican War veterans and, for a few years at least, an occasional, shuffling old-timer from the War of 1812, and finally, splendid in their visored caps and coats, the Civil War veterans. At midday came the patriotic speeches. And afterward, while children raced underfoot, the elders gossiped over fried chicken, homemade pickles, and angel-food cake eaten on broad-planked tables set up on the town common.

Throughout these extravagant celebrations there was always the nagging counterpoint of moralistic preaching. Before each holiday feast, Americans were sternly reminded by their clergy that they should share with less fortunate neighbors. Newspapers and magazines were full of editorial scoldings: Christmas gifts had become too lavish, Easter parades too gaudy. Americans suffered suitable guilt and struggled to reconcile the doctrine of deprivation with their own need to bust loose once in a while. But it was a case of protesting too much. The fact was that in this era, holidays were a particular lot of fun.

Holiday postcard

Hand-tinted
calling card

Gentleman's
calling card

The New Year

In the late 1800s the great New Year's rite was not a big party the night before, but quieter customs on the day itself. During the '70s single gentlemen armed with fancy calling cards went on a round of visits to ladies of their acquaintance, aided by local newspapers, which printed long lists of damsels who would be "at home" to such callers. But by 1880 bachelors had so abused the custom ("This is my 47th call!" shouted one swain on the run) that it died of social disapproval. Married men, however, continued to observe the day, either by taking their families to fancy restaurants or by going calling *en famille*—a practice that, like bachelor calling, did not always fall within the bounds of etiquette (*below*).

Proper Calling

Ladies expecting calls on New Year's should be in readiness to receive from 10 a.m. to 9 p.m. Upon calling, the gentlemen are invited to remove overcoat and hat, which invitation is accepted unless it is the design to make the call very brief. Gloves are sometimes retained upon the hand during the call, but this is optional. The call should not exceed ten or fifteen minutes, unless it is mutually agreeable to prolong the stay. The ladies should have a bright, cheerful fire and a table, conveniently located in the room, with refreshments, consisting of fruits, cakes, bread and other food, such as may be deemed desirable. No intoxicating drinks should be allowed.

Improper Calling

Disagreeable callers are the husband and wife who come with a child and a small dog; the husband making himself familiar with the hostess, the dog barking at the cat, the child taking free run of the house, while the wife passes around the room, handling and examining the ornaments.

Some evening callers make themselves odious by continuing their visit too long, and even when they have risen to depart they lack decision to go but will stand several minutes before taking final leave, and then when wraps are on, will tell one more story while the hostess protects herself as best she can from the incoming gusts of wind and storm, sometimes thus taking a cold that ends in death. When the guest is ready to go—go.
–Manual of Social and Business Forms, 1873

Valentine's Day

A sentimental holiday like Valentine's Day called forth, naturally, the most dewy effusions, as saccharine cards designed in the most elaborate shapes, and adorned with ribbons, blossoms, fringes and bows, transmitted the seasonal message of love in glorious papier-mâché. In an effort to stem the flow of treacle, magazines like *Harper's (below)* might sniff at the vulgarization of the valentine custom, but in vain. The high priestess of the cult of complex valentines was a genteel Mount Holyoke graduate, Esther Howland of Worcester, Massachusetts, whose lacy handmade creations sold for as much as $50. Alas, though her valentine messages helped the romantic lives of many others, they did not benefit Esther herself; she died unmarried.

Fold-out seal

Requiem for St. Valentine

The spirit and sentiment of St. Valentine's Day are fading. The world is growing too prosaic. Lovemaking and matrimony are no longer conducted on the principle of a bashful lover worshipping from afar off, and under the disguise of some incognito, some shrinking maiden who revels in the mystery of an unknown adorer. Marriage is walked up to by both parties in a businesslike fashion. Neither is in the least timid, and the matter is put through according to rule, and as if it wore only the features of an ordinary contract. This has nearly done away with the occupation of good St. Valentine, and the missives he now presides over are too often only annoying communications, and sent by persons who have no regard for the feelings of others. His fairy gifts, his turtle doves and tender verses have been nearly hustled off our soil by a struggle to adapt him to the customs of our commercial country and make him pay.

Clearly it is impossible to expect that delicate or sensitive people can hereafter make use of the valentine. There seems nothing to do but resign it with a sigh as one more of the pleasant customs of our forefathers, which for some reason we have concluded to abandon.
—*Harper's Weekly,* February 21, 1880

Valentine fan

Candy heart, 1890

promise
to be true

Then
come what may
I'll be for aye
over fond to
you.

Have kindly thoughts
of me

Calling card

Candy-box card

POPPING THE QUESTION.

Comic valentine

A Gift
of Love

Fold-out valentine

Trinket box

Notepaper

Easter

In the first 60 years of the century, Easter was little celebrated in the United States. The country's Protestant majority scorned the day as papist, though during the Civil War some communities had set it aside as a day of mourning for fallen soldiers. In the post-war years, however, Easter suddenly emerged as a favored holiday. Youngsters took up those ancient Easter symbols, the egg and the rabbit, and in 1878 President Hayes inaugurated the annual Easter egg roll on the White House lawn. Gentlemen sent cards to ladies. And both sexes turned the holiday into a fashion show, as people of all shapes and tastes paraded their brightest spring outfits up and down the main streets of their towns.

An Appeal for Elegance
Everybody is young on Easter Sunday. Matrons throw off their staid airs, and old men rustle bravely. But may Life be permitted one suggestion. Year after year, the homeliest people have inevitably appeared Easter Sunday in the most conspicuous of garments, thus attracting special attention to their lack of natural attractions. If the homely people would either stay home tomorrow or, if they venture out, array themselves in proper garments, the symphonic essence of the street parade would better be preserved.
–Brooklyn Life, April 5, 1890

Three-dimensional card

Molded–plaster candy box

Easter greeting cards

Millinery trade card

Gift Easter eggs

Die-cut Easter seals

Independence Day

The loudest, most bumptious holi-day of all was the Fourth of July. Every town throughout America had its patriotic parade, accompanied by a cacophony of brass bands, booming fireworks, sham battles, and flag-draped oratory—often heavily political in content. Yet while most of the nation was hailing Old Glory, the flag was also being desecrated and bitterly fought over. Advertisers and politicians overprinted slogans and pictures upon it. In the heat of partisan battles, the flag was torn, and shots were even fired in real anger *(below),* giving an unwelcome tinge of realism to the raucous cannonading on the glorious Fourth of July.

In Defense of Old Glory
Southport, Conn., July 2—I write, as chairman of the flag committee of the Connecticut Daugh-ters of the Revolution, to tell you of the work we are doing to foster a feeling of loyalty to the flag that has been honored and guarded in weary marches and perilous voyages. We need such an education of public sentiment as will loyally sup-port righteous legislation for the purpose of enforcing respect for Old Glory.

It should hardly be a question of argument whether a man may wantonly and maliciously tear our country's flag into shreds or trample it; hardly less a question whether it ought to be used as a vehicle of advertisement for nostrums or liquors; yet instances of such misuse are too well known.

A stranger in Council Bluffs, Ia., rode up to a large American flag bearing a partisan banner

Fourth of July parade in Evanston, Illinois

Postcard

Song sheet

Program poster, 1879

and fired upon it with a shotgun. A soldier shot at the mounted assailant, killing the horse and wounding the man, who escaped.

At Sedalia, Mo., a child was singing campaign songs and holding a flag in her hands. The flag was seized by a man of the opposing party and thrown upon a bonfire, and its destruction applauded by companions.

Clubs of oppositional political parties met at the railway station at Janesville, Wis., with the result that the national flag was rotten-egged and torn.

A procession marched through the streets of Lafayette, Ill., bearing the red flag at the front and trailing the American flag after it through the filth of the street.

We want the flag protected from all insults. We appeal to loyal Americans to stand by the DAR in this crusade.

–Rebekah W. P. Nulkeley, July 3, 1898

The Fourth in Philadelphia

4:37 a.m. Sunrise Salute to Old Glory. Battery A, Nat'l Guard, 44 guns.

9 a.m. Celebration: Invocation, Reading of the Declaration, Oration.

10 a.m. Sham Battle, First Brigade, Penna. National Guard. About 40,000 rounds of ammunition will be expended. Naval Battalion will add to the din by the discharge of boat howitzers.

1 p.m. Field Sports. A special feature will be an Exhibition by the German Turnvereins of Philadelphia.

2:30 p.m. Grand Balloon Ascension with 13 hot-air balloons, symbolic of the original colonies.

2:30 p.m.–6:00 p.m. Rowing Races.

8:30 p.m. Grand Pyrotechnic Display.

–Souvenir program

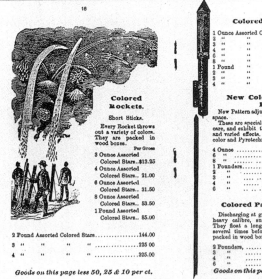

Fireworks catalog

Patriotic doll

Halloween and Thanksgiving

Americans of the ultrarespectable Victorian era thoroughly relished the old pagan holidays of Halloween and Thanksgiving. Halloween, which had begun as a druidic rite complete with moonlit blood offerings, had turned by the late 1880s in the United States into a young people's holiday. It still catered enthusiastically to superstition, but of a mild parlor variety, such as the quaint rituals at left, below, to indicate whether

Stereopticon slide

Mirrors of Love

A quaint method of determining the faithfulness of lovers is to put three nuts upon the bars of stove grates, naming the nuts after the lovers. If a nut cracks or jumps the lover will prove unfaithful; if it begins to blaze and burn, he has a regard for the person making the trial. If the nuts named after the girl and her lover burn together, they will be married. The reading of the nuts may prove for many a lad and lassie a true prophecy.

Here is another device: Take three dishes, put clean water in one, foul water in another, leave the third empty. Blindfold a person and lead him to where the dishes are ranged; he or she dips the left hand—if by chance in the clean water the future husband or wife will come to the bar of matrimony a bachelor or maid—if in the foul, a widower or widow; if in the empty dish it foretells no marriage at all. It is repeated three times and each time the arrangement of the dishes is altered. The old test of

Cardboard party decoration

putting apple seeds on the eyes or cheeks and naming them after swains is another practice. The most faithful is he who sticks the longest.

But it is the maid with the stoutest heart who fears not her fate—and whose desires are great—who dares put it to the touch of the cellar stairs' visit at midnight. The proper form is for her to let down her back hair, then "dressed all in white" with uplifted candle, à la Lady Macbeth, in the left hand a mirror, she proceeds to wend her way slowly—and alone—down the stairs backward to the cellar; it is then when the final step is reached and the critical and dramatic moment arrives, that she will see the pictured face of her future husband in the mirror she carries in her left hand. It is only for those possessing great faith that the face in the mirror will materialize. If the maiden reading this doesn't believe in the efficacy of this special rite, let her try it for herself—seeing is believing.

–The Ladies World, November 1892

girl would get boy. Thanksgiving was America's version of the harvest festivals of the ancient Semitic tribes. The celebration was confined mainly to New England until 1863, when it grew into the all-American feasting day, complete with lavish dinner recipes and lavish reminders *(below)* about the tribulations of less fortunate folk and the virtues of both humility and generosity on this day of plenty.

Thanksgiving postcard

Classroom Thanksgiving

Thanksgiving Sermon

Many men today, sitting in the darkness of great calamity, need some public summons to thanksgiving, lest they forget that they have anything to be thankful for. There are proud, rich men whose riches have gone down in disaster and they know not which way to turn, with families, reared in luxury, clinging to them for elegant support. And there are poor, working men, honest, sturdy, out of work, in rickety hovels and garrets with scanty fires, who go in tatters and eat the meat of charity or chance or none.

And there are women who, with sick and hungry children, tremble at the coming of brutal, drunken husbands. Ah, these days of thanksgiving are, to them, horribly misnamed—gloomy, gloomy days, and full of grim visions. And there is many a desolate work-girl, in our cities, weary but not of labor, who shudders, standing near to hunger and there sees the smiling face of the tempter as he reaches out for her—how persuasively—furs and fires and food, comfort, luxury, and sin. Can these give thanks just now at the behest of our proclamations? Yet let us hail this day with thanksgiving, remembering that though there is no perfect day this side heaven, there is no rayless night except beyond the grave.

–The Reverend A. S. Fiske, San Francisco

Thanksgiving Menu
Raw Oysters.
Boiled Rockfish, Egg Sauce.
Potato Balls.
Roasted Turkey, Stuffing, Giblet Gravy.
Browned Sweet Potatoes.
Baked Squash.
Cranberry Jelly. Sour Grape Jelly.
Moulded Spinach.
Venison Pasty.
Ham Baked in Cider, and Garnished.
Mince Pies. Pumpkin Pies. Fruit.
Coffee. Hygeia Sparkling Lithia Water.
–The Ladies World, November 1892

Christmas

An occasion of literally delirious joy" was Teddy Roosevelt's description of Christmas in the 1870s. T.R.'s comment was in keeping with the refulgent style of the Victorian Christmas. But equally in keeping with the spirit of Victorian times was the counterpoint to all this opulence—an overdose of morality that directed thoughts to the meaning of Christmas, with references to the deserving poor and the widow's plight. The English author Charles Dickens's moralistic *A Christmas Carol* swept the nation; and when Dickens read his *Carol* on one of his several visits to the U.S., he reported afterward that "one girl burst into a passion of grief about Tiny Tim and had to be taken out."

Tasteful Giving

It takes common sense and independence to accept a costly present from a rich friend, without making any return.

If you have money to spend on presents, do not waste on people richer than yourself, but on those poorer.

Above all, in sending presents do not send articles that cost money and are vulgar and tawdry. A piece of music, a note written on Christmas Day, wishing many happy returns, or a few flowers, entail no obligation, require no work, and do their own work of love as well as costly gifts, and show a delicacy of breeding.
—*The Ladies World*, December 1892

The Greedy Wife

"Would you have me steal to provide you with the means of gratifying your desire to make expensive presents?" a young man only three years married asked his wife last Christmas. "I would have you support me in the manner to which I have been accustomed," was the unwifely rejoinder. That night the young man went out. The next day he could not be found but later he was escorted to his home by his broken-hearted father who found him in some out of the way place recovering from his first alcoholic spree. "This is your work," the old man said to his daughter-in-law and never were words more deserved. It was her work that her husband cares no more for her; her work that she is unhappy; her work that her husband's ambition is dead. It was impossible to satisfy her when he did his best; consequently further effort was useless. Reflect upon these things.
—*The Ladies World*, December 1892

Christmas card

Handmade
Christmas stocking

Christmas sticker

Christmas toy

Child's scrapbook

Cycling

★

A NATION HITS THE ROAD

Florida wheelmen take a break on the road near Tallahassee.

America Goes A-Wheeling

In 1876, when Philadelphia put on its dazzling exhibition to celebrate the 100th birthday of the United States, the millions of people who came to gaze at the scientific wonders displayed there gave only passing notice to the bicycle showcased by the British firm of Smith & Starley. After all, bicycles had been around in one form or another for most of the century. And to the visitors at Philadelphia, Smith & Starley's "ordinary English bicycle"—called "the ordinary" for short—with a saddled front wheel five feet high and an 18-inch rear wheel for balance, did not seem all that different.

Yet in the America of 1876, the bicycle was clearly an idea whose time had come. At least so it appeared to a Bostonian named Colonel Albert A. Pope, who converted his air-pistol factory into a pioneering bicycle works, and then saw his business quickly climb above a million dollars per annum. Within eight years there were 50,000 cyclists wheeling around the United States.

In 1885, the British produced a second cycling coup by introducing their low-wheeled "safety," a bicycle that balanced on two smaller, equal-sized wheels and was much easier to ride than the ordinary. Almost overnight, the bicycle became a national craze. During the decade of the 1890s some 10 million Americans took to the wheel. By 1896 bike manufacturing was a $60 million business in the United States, complete with ads of all sorts (*above, left and inset*) to fan the flames of consumer interest. The Pope Manufacturing Company was turning out a cycle a minute at an average price of $100. Riders spent another $12 million a year for spare parts and fancy extras—lamps, bells, cyclometers, and that ultimate in accessories, according to an ad in *Bicycling World*, "A Good Thing for Bicycle Rider; Iver Johnson Cycle Revolver."

> "We claim a great utility that daily must increase; / We claim from inactivity a sensible release; / A constant mental, physical, and moral help we feel, / That bids us turn enthusiasts, and cry, 'God bless the wheel!'"

Poet Will Carleton, circa 1890

Elegant cyclist Maurice Aron shows off the costume that won him the first-place wreath in the New York Evening Telegram's 1896 parade.

A tricycle built for two

Nattily capped quadricycle riders

Setting out on a quadricycle

High Wheels and High Fashion

One of the favored diversions of nineteenth century cyclists was touring. Around Boston, for example, where the first cycling club was organized in the 1870s, scarcely a weekend passed without groups of strong-legged wheelmen taking a century tour, that is, 50 miles out on Saturday, and 50 miles back on Sunday. Ladies toured in a more leisurely fashion, traveling on tandem tricycles or quadricycles. Besides being splendid exercise, these mixed outings afforded an opportunity for a stylish young matron to display her sportiest fashions on a kind of freewheeling *concours d'élégance*.

A typical tour-cum-fashion-show was the Ladies' North Shore Tricycle outing from Malden to Gloucester, Massachusetts, which began on October 6, 1887, and encompassed four pleasure-filled days. An account of the gala send-off, along with a preview of the tour itself, appeared *(below)* in the Malden, Massachusetts, *Evening Mail.*

Malden, Oct. 6—This morning the third annual ladies' tricycle tour was started. By the appointed time, the bicyclists had assembled on Salem Street in front of the Public Library, where a large number of people had gathered to see the start. The lady bicyclists looked very "nifty," in their natty costumes and tourist caps, and were the objects of admiring glances from the lookers-on. Following is the program.

First day, Thursday, Oct. 6—Leave Malden Square at 9:50 a.m., ride to Salem (11½ miles), dinner at Essex House at 12 M. Leave Salem at 1:30 and ride to Gloucester, around Cape Ann (15½ miles), supper and lodging at Pavilion. Ride of first day, 27 miles.

Second day, Friday, Oct. 7—Start at 9 a.m. around Cape Ann. A picnic lunch will be served on the rocks at Pigeon Cove. Six o'clock dinner and lodging at Pavilion. Ride of second day, 17 miles.

Third day, Saturday, Oct. 8—Start at 9 a.m. Ride to Magnolia (4½ miles) and visit Rafe's Chasm, Norman's Woe, etc. Dinner at Willow Cottage. Ride to Salem (13½ miles). Supper and lodging at Essex House. Ride of third day, 17½ miles.

Fourth day, Sunday, Oct. 9—Leave Essex House at 9 a.m. Ride to Marblehead Neck and Nahant, stopping a short time at each place. Dinner at Nahant, 12 M. The homeward run to suit the pleasure of the party. Ride of fourth day, 10 miles.

A musical and literary program has been arranged for Friday evening at the Pavilion in Gloucester, where professional and amateur talent will entertain the company. Pleasure will be the order of the day and riding will be done in easy stages, giving time to enjoy nature's beauties.

Many wheelmen and ladies will undoubtedly run down Saturday night or Sunday morning to meet the party and participate in the homeward run.

*Mr. and Mrs. William Quinnell of Chelsea,
Massachusetts, wore matching blue and white, with
Mr. Quinnell in velvet knickers and blue socks.*

Day at the Races

In 1875 a small English cycling magazine called *Ixion* announced a two-wheeler race meet. Prizes were offered—for professionals, 20 pounds; for amateurs, 12 guineas. Like the cycle itself, bike racing and bike magazines soon caught the sporting fancy of America.

In the fall of 1883, Springfield, Massachusetts, staged the first recorded U.S. cycling championship. By the time the decade ended, crowds of 25,000 were watching outdoor races like the one at right in Buffalo. Indoor ovals in Philadelphia, Chicago and New York annually outdrew the local major-league ball clubs with special speed trials and six-day endurance contests from which the winners took home purses of as much as $15,000 a year. By 1897 racing had become such a craze that it prompted one national magazine to scold: "The question of Sunday bicycle-racing is again being agitated. It should be prohibited. The spectators of Sunday bicycle-racing are not the class which stands for law and order."

But no one paid much attention. In fact, the nation's fascination with cycling speed reached its peak two years later when slim, wiry Charles Murphy went roaring down a board track behind a railroad train filled with newsmen to become the first human to cycle a measured mile in less than 60 seconds. At the finish, Murphy collapsed, gasping, "Carry me back to where my wife is." Instead he was taken to the waiting crowd, which hailed the newly crowned "Mile-a-Minute Murphy" as a sportsman to rank with Gentleman Jim Corbett among contemporary U.S. heroes.

Spectators swarm around the starters of the 1894 Martin Road Race, a 25-mile amateur event held in Buffalo, New York.

Occupations

★

Puddlers and water boys gather outside an Ohio steel mill.

The Many Roads to Riches

During the enormous geographic and economic expansion in the decades after the Civil War, Americans found before them the greatest array of job opportunities in the history of any nation. Not only was there the better part of a rich continent to cultivate, but the climax of the industrial revolution had also opened up thousands of jobs in new areas of technology.

In 1870, for example, there was no such thing as a telephone. But by 1900 there were 19,000 telephone operators. The booming U.S. iron and steel industry had put more than a million people to work turning out nearly half the world's supply of structural metals. And clothing factories, expanded during the Civil War to turn out soldiers' uniforms, converted so successfully to the mass production of civilian clothes that at century's end 1.45 million people were employed in the business.

Though the incipient American labor movement was beginning to flex its muscles, many workers were not bothered by the fact that most of this labor was for coolie wages: seven out of 10 industrial workers earned no more than 10 cents an hour. For in keeping with the stern ethics of the era, most Americans willingly lived by a hard-driving, self-abnegating work philosophy. Besides, in the laissez-faire business atmosphere of the day, there was the chance for any kid—at least any white kid—to do as Andrew Carnegie had done: starting as a bobbin boy at age 13 in a textile mill, he had wound up as the richest steelman on earth.

Women, too, were seizing new opportunities en masse; by 1890 some 3,704,000 of them were in the U.S. labor force. Even more significant, seven out of every 10 colleges had gone coeducational by the turn of the century, and they had graduated 7,500 woman doctors, 3,000 ministers, and 1,000 lawyers.

The lack of child-labor laws also meant that some 1.75 million kids under 15 were out scratching in mines and tobacco fields for as little as 25 cents a day. But this, too, was thought good and proper, according to a slogan of the day: "The factories need the children and the children need the factories." For this was America's greatest time of growth. Anybody could see that. And an observer could see, too, by the prideful bearing of the workers, that what Americans wanted was to get on with the job.

Farmers in Oregon finish stacking a pile of straw thrown out by their steam thresher. This device, along with other farm machinery that was invented during the era, helped double American corn and wheat production between 1860 and 1880; the total doubled again by the end of the century.

The cowboy tended and drove to shipping centers the vast herds of cattle raised on the western plains in the last third of the nineteenth century. Some 40,000 of these hard-riding nomads, of whom 5,000 were black, drove their beef great distances—often more than 1,000 parched, dangerous miles—to the meat markets in Kansas City and Chicago, where the cattle were sold and slaughtered. By 1890 the railroad was taking over the cowboy's job of moving cattle long distances, which forced many of the black cowboys to take new jobs with the competition as Pullman porters.

A newspaper publisher, Colonel John P. Jackson, shown here with a folded copy of his own San Francisco Daily Evening Post, was one of hundreds of journalistic entrepreneurs who profited from the nation's growth. With the extension of the railroad and the settling of the West, the number of daily newspapers jumped from 971 to 1,610 between 1880 and 1890, and total U.S. circulation of papers went from 3.6 million to 8.4 million.

A sheep herder displays the pelts of coyotes he shot with his 1873 model Winchester rifle in an effort to shield his Montana flock from predators. Sheep raising in Victorian America was big business—and very good business, too. In 1870 there were no fewer than 80 sheep for every 100 humans in the population as a whole. Any young man with a few dollars could get a start at raising sheep; a pair could be bought for $3.74, and a healthy pair could be expected to proliferate fast. Two men in California who began with a herd of 18,900 in 1866 had 58,000 ten years later.

A surveyor, this man was one of the many who went all over the United States with their transits in the last third of the century. They laid out sections and properties in the eight new states, totaling 733,676 square miles, that were admitted to the Union. Surveyors also ran lines for 64,186 miles of railroad put down in the same period.

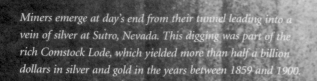

Miners emerge at day's end from their tunnel leading into a vein of silver at Sutro, Nevada. This digging was part of the rich Comstock Lode, which yielded more than half a billion dollars in silver and gold in the years between 1859 and 1900.

Telephone linemen in New England's Connecticut River Valley festoon one of the millions of poles erected during the last three decades of the century. In 1876 there were only 3,000 telephones in the entire nation; by 1900 there were 1.4 million.

Overleaf: Hops pickers show off their abundant harvest on an upstate New York farm in the 1880s. About half a pound of hops went into the making of a barrel of beer, the favorite drink of the American male. In 1900 national consumption totaled 34.3 million barrels, or 16 gallons per capita.

Milk delivery

Furniture moving

Coal delivery

Veterinary ambulance

Wagoners transported virtually every kind of shorthaul load in the United States—and before the nation's rail network was substantially completed, they moved a great deal of the long-distance freight as well. In 1884 the country had 15.4 million horses, and as these pictures show, they brought the day's supply of milk, carried furniture across town, delivered meat in refrigerated wagons, and sometimes transported ailing horses from the barn to the veterinarian's hospital. Even the heaviest commodities moved by horse power; it took two tons of coal to keep a moderate-sized house warm for a few months in winter, and wagons like the one above delivered it right to the cellar door.

The blacksmith and his backhander—an aide or apprentice who stood behind the smith and handed over tools as needed—were essential members of every community. In 1900 some 226,477 of them throughout the United States shod the horses that transported Americans and their goods. In addition, blacksmiths manufactured nails, scythes, harness fastenings, pots and pans, plowshares, and sometimes even swords.

Education

★

DRILL, DRILL, DRILL

Grade-school children sit glumly in their Valley Falls, Kansas, classroom.

The Ladder of Learning

A buoyant belief in the power of education sprang up in post–Civil War days and swept all segments of the country. Plutocrats like Andrew Carnegie, small-town farmers, city dwellers, and professional educators all felt that their personal versions of the American dream would come true just as soon as the blessing of learning was available to anyone at any level. In the three decades after the war, 31 state legislatures saw to it that little children received this blessing, whether they wanted it or not, by passing laws making attendance compulsory at elementary schools. As a result, by 1898 some 15 million youngsters were in school learning their bedrock three R's—plus an occasional so-called expression subject such as music or art. And urged on by the unsparing rod of straight-eyed schoolmarms and masters, they also learned the rules and rewards of decorous classroom behavior (*page 119*).

As the youngsters moved upward, they created a heavy demand for more public high schools, which were sometimes called people's colleges. "The high school," one educator pontificated, "is the institution which shall level the distinction between the rich and the poor," thus allowing the laborer's boy to "stand alongside the rich man's son." Between 1870 and 1900 the number of these levelers for the laborer's child burgeoned from about 500 to 6,000. Higher education as well was undergoing a period of growth. In 1862 Congress passed the Morrill Act, giving enormous federal tracts to each state for the establishment of colleges of agricultural and mechanical arts. By the end of the century, there were 977 colleges of all kinds, serving 238,000 students. It was at the college level, too, that the wealthy industrial barons were most involved, for sound practical reasons that glared unmistakably through the soft glow of philanthropy. Carnegie, for one, was certain that the best way to sustain the workers' faith in the capitalistic system was to provide "ladders upon which the aspiring can rise." And what better ladder, asked Carnegie, than a college education?

Putting his money where his morality was, Carnegie handed out $20 million to various freshwater colleges, and in 1900 spent $2 million to start Pittsburgh's Carnegie Institute of Technology. Other tycoons fell in step, among them Baltimore banker Johns Hopkins, Western Union founder Ezra Cornell, California railroad-builder Leland Stanford, and oil baron John D. Rockefeller, who underwrote a Baptist university the church fathers called Chicago when the tycoon forbade them to name it after him.

"Just see, wherever we peer into the first tiny springs of the national life, how this true panacea for all the ills of the body politic bubbles forth—education, education, education."

Andrew Carnegie,
Triumphant Democracy, 1886

A Cornell graduate dons his mortarboard, armed with the college degree that one in 400 Americans had in 1900.

Practice Makes Perfect

For Victorian children, grade school was a robot parade ground for the mind; virtually everything was drilled into young heads through interminable repetition. One approved method for teaching arithmetic required that the pupils spend the entire first year working only on the numbers 1 through 10—counting, adding, multiplying—before they were permitted to advance to the lofty plateau of 11 through 20. Reading and spelling *(page 116)* were much the same. And even handwriting was turned into a mechanistic nightmare, with drill books that told precisely where the pupil must place his thumb, fingers, and even his feet before he was permitted to start.

> "In the training of children it is better to do one thing one hundred times, than one hundred things one time."
>
> Education axiom

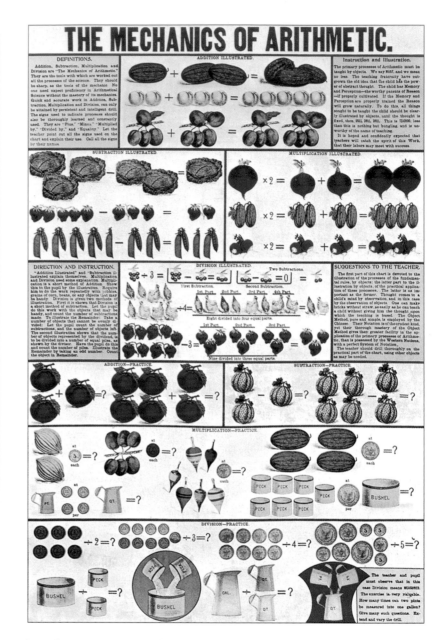

Arithmetic

This arithmetic chart, one of a series offered by a Minneapolis publisher, taught elementary math using objects that were most familiar to school kids in an America where farming was still the major occupation. One Kansas pupil remembered "a teacher who explained common fractions by an apple neatly cut into segments. I really understood fractions for the first time that day." Nevertheless, most kids still hated arithmetic. Small wonder. Added to the innate horror of basic math were exhortations like the one on the chart above: "DRILL, DRILL, DRILL."

A Arm your mind against any temptation. A

B Better have no company than bad company. B

B Better have no company than bad company B

C Contentment is more to be desired than riches. C

Key to Correct Pen-Holding.

1. Put the *forefinger* flat upon the barrel of the pen-holder.
2. Put the *second finger* nail under the pen-holder.
3. Put the upper corner of the *thumb nail* against the pen-holder, opposite the 1st joint of the forefinger.
4. Bend the joints of the thumb outward.
5. Keep the pen-holder *up* against the side of the forefinger.
6. Keep the forefinger *straightened*.
7. Keep the wrist straight and off the desk or book.
8. Keep both points of the pen on the paper alike.
9. Keep the top of the pen-holder pointing to the right shoulder.
10. Keep the arms and paper in line.

D Deserve success and you shall command it D

Penmanship

Military precision in all aspects of penmanship was emphasized in illustrations (left) from the top-selling instruction books of an Ohio clerk named Platt Rogers Spencer. His jealous imitators hewed to the same principles and the same lettering forms; for example, one copybook (inset above) advertised "75 percent more practice than Spencerian," a point much in the imitator's favor.

Right-side position   Front position

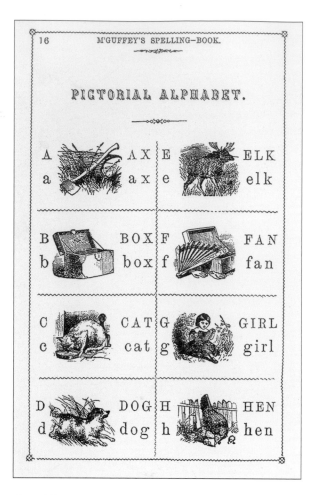

LESSON XI.

ī'ron (ī'urn)
eÿe' lĭd̥s
fōrge
in tĕnse'

clĭn'ker ty
shrĭnk
lā'bor
hăm'mer

THE BLACKSMITH.

1. Clink, clink, clinkerty clink!
   We begin to hammer at morning's blink,
     And hammer away
     Till the busy day,
  Like us, aweary, to rest shall sink.

2. Clink, clink, clinkerty clink!
  From labor and care we never will shrink;
     But our fires we'll blow
     Till our forges glow
  With light intense, while our eyelids wink.

Spelling

America's best-selling schoolbooks, McGuffey's Readers, sold over 60 million readers and spellers from 1870 to 1890. The skills taught were strongly stressed in a semi-literate society. One former pupil remembered losers in a spelling bee at his grammar school "shuffling downwards, with eyes on their toes."

Reading

As early as 1887 McGuffey's publisher put out a series of revised editions that featured attractive illustrations. Engravings like the one above, from the Third Eclectic Reader, typified this effort to give schoolbooks visual appeal. But the style of accompanying prose remained cheerily, drearily the same.

Elocution

In the 1870s oral reading developed—or deteriorated—into a posturing form of expression called elocution. This bizarre exercise concentrated on dramatic presentation of the written word, using a spectrum of set-piece poses to emphasize various phrases in a memorized passage. An 1874 manual for high-school speakers (right) showed some of the various positions that were de rigueur for public recitations; Mark Twain scornfully described them as "the painfully exact and spasmodic gestures which a machine might have used."

"Wisest, brightest"   "Meanest of mankind"   "Heir of glory"   "Frail child of dust!"

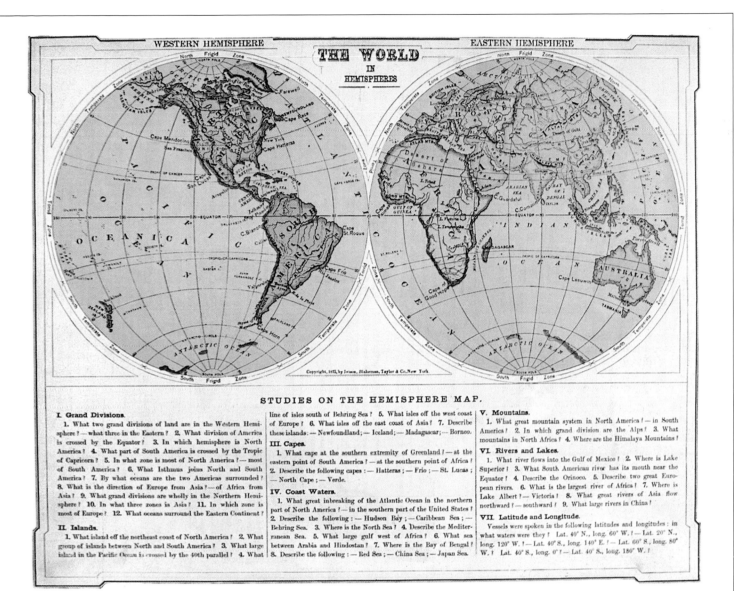

Geography

In an 1875 grade school, Manhattan youngsters studied the world from this map in Swinton's A Complete Course in Geography.

"Look there!" "The fatal blow" "Oh, despair!" "Lifteth to heaven" "This vast galaxy"

History

The story of the Declaration of Independence was told with un-Victorian simplicity in G.P. Quackenbos's American History for Schools (below), published in 1877. But Custer's Last Stand is described in the same book with the more familiar hyperbole: "'The White Chief' undauntedly defended himself with his sword, until a bullet laid him in the dust."

The Declaration of Independence

Congress began to think of renouncing allegiance to the crown. In June, Richard Henry Lee introduced a resolution: "That these united colonies are, and of right ought to be, free and independent states; and that their political connection with Great Britain is, and ought to be, dissolved." A committee of five was appointed to draft a formal Declaration of Independence. This document was written by Thomas Jefferson, and received a few alterations from John Adams and Franklin, of the committee. It was presented to Congress July 1st, and after being carefully considered and amended was passed on the 4th of July—ever since observed as the birthday of American freedom. The bell of the old state-house, in which Congress was assembled, rang out the glad tidings. The people, south and north, hailed the news with delight, kindling bonfires, illuminating their houses, and receiving the Declaration, as read by their orators, with heart-stirring acclamations.

Music

When the music reader below was published in 1888, rote singing as a form of stiff-necked classroom recreation was giving way to an effort to teach sight-reading of sheet music as part of a more flexible elementary school curriculum.

THIS

Testimonial of Merit

IS AWARDED TO

Samuel M. Landsmann

For punctuality, deportment, and diligent attention to study during the past 6 *months at*

SCHOOL

Grammar No. 13

R. A. Barry, Chm'n   *J. C. Wagner, Sec.*

H. C. Litchfield, Principal.

New York, July 1st 1880

Having stoically and decorously endured another school year of rote and routine, a 10-year-old New Yorker came home with this reward.

Against a blackboard display of handwriting and arithmetic, grade schoolers in Keota, Iowa, celebrate the last day of school.

NEW YORK JOURNA

SAMPSON SILENCED SAN JUAN; NOW SEEKS SPANISH FLE

Crowds throng New York's Newspaper Row during the Spanish-American War, 1898.

> "Accuracy! Accuracy is to a newspaper what virtue is to a woman."
>
> Joseph Pulitzer to his staff

Joseph Pulitzer

William R. Hearst

Hearst's version of the Spanish surrender led off with a hand-drawn, four-inch, screamer headline that topped Pulitzer's paper on the stands.

From Good Gray to Dirty Yellow

In 1883 Hungarian-born Joseph Pulitzer, age 36, came to the big city from St. Louis and bought the New York *World,* which did not seem to be much of a bargain—its circulation was only 15,000 and it was losing $40,000 a year. But Pulitzer did not seem to be much of a bargain himself—six feet, two and a half inches tall, thin as a rake, with a large bladelike nose, a receding chin, and such poor eyesight that he would soon need a keeper. It would have taken a perceptive person to recognize Pulitzer for what he would become: the best journalist of the nineteenth century.

When Pulitzer emerged on the New York scene, the traditional American newspaper, dull in appearance and rarely selling more than 200,000 copies a day, was being drastically remodeled. In part the change was taking place because 1870 to 1900 was a bully time for news, much of it of the terrible sort that publishers relish: the assassination of President Garfield, the Johnstown flood, Custer's annihilation, the Charleston earthquake, the Spanish-American War. Events of that caliber stimulated the headline writers; some of them clung to the narrow, many-decked old style that, because of its visual effect, was called a tombstone. But by 1898, on the day after the American defeat of the Spanish fleet at Manila Bay, the *New York Journal,* the paper owned by Pulitzer's cheeky new challenger, William Randolph Hearst, splattered a single word, "SURRENDERS!" across all seven columns of its front page.

On his first day as owner of the *World,* Pulitzer assembled the staff and said, "Gentlemen, heretofore you have all been living in the parlor and taking baths every day. Now I wish you to understand that, in future, you are all walking down the Bowery." Himself an immigrant and an earnest believer in democracy, he saw that there were millions of other immigrants, poor people crammed into the slums of New York, who had no paper to speak for them. As Pulitzer made plain in his opening editorial: "There is room in this great and growing city for a journal that is not only cheap [two cents] but bright, not only bright but large, not only large but truly democratic—dedicated to the cause of the people rather than to that of the purse potentates—devoted more to the news of the New than the Old World—that will expose all fraud and sham, fight all public evils and abuses—that will serve and battle for the people."

NIGHT SPECIAL. SATURDAY'S 1,408,200 CIRCULATION.

NEW YORK EVENING JOURNAL WAR

NO. 5,646—P. M.   NEW YORK, MONDAY, MAY 2, 1898.   PRICE ONE CENT

SURRENDERS!

DEWEY'S FLEET TAKES MANILA.

THE SPANISH FLAGSHIP ON FIRE.

WASHINGTON GETS NEWS OF THE CITY'S FALL

WASHINGTON, MAY 2.---IT IS REPORTED THAT AMBASSADOR HAY THROUGH THE MEDIUM OF THE BRITISH FOREIGN OFFICE HAS SECURED NEWS OF THE SURRENDER OF MANILA, BUT CONFIRMATION OF THIS REPORT CANNOT BE MADE. THE STATE DEPARTMENT SAYS THAT IT HAS NOT RECEIVED OFFICIAL NOTICE AND SEC'Y LONG OF THE NAVY IS ALSO WITHOUT DEFINITE NEWS.

When the cable service from Manila ceased the city was being bombarded.

Official reports to Great Britain announce that the Spanish fleet at Manila was annihilated.

Admiral Montijo admits that his fleet has been demolished.

Madrid has been declared under martial law.

Don Juan de Austria was blown up.

AND THEY GOT IT AS DEMANDED.

struggle will be short and decisive. The God
will give no care as brill'   complete as
demand—

THE HOME COMING.

WHEN THIS CRUEL WAR IS OVER.

In the middle of the fight, the Spaniards say,

Dewey's squadron entered Manila Bay at night. Fighting began in early morning.

Spanish Admiral deserted his flagship, Maria Cristina, then on fire.

Captain Cadarso, commander of the Spanish flagship, was killed.

Besides fighting the enemy's ship, American forces sustained a hot fire from Spanish forts.

PRAYER OF THANKS IN THE SENATE

Washington, May 2.—The chaplain's opening prayer in the Senate was a paen of triumph for the great victory of the American fleet. These are his words:

"We give Thee hearty thanks for the good news coming to us across the sea of the success with which Thou art crowning the discipline and value of the officers and men of our Asiatic squadron.

"We bless Thee for the magnificent and unexampled..."

Pulitzer scrupulously printed the important news and played it straight. He also printed sharp, bitter stories of life in the slums calculated to provoke honest wrath: "She had lain down in the cellar to sleep, and the sewer that runs under the house overflowed and suffocated her where she lay. No one will ever know who killed Kate Sweeny. No one will ever summon the sanitary inspectors. Nobody seems to have thought it worth an investigation." There were other items in the *World*'s news columns, however, that did not appear to have been published by the same man. Pulitzer, who was not a great innovator but a master synthesist, had observed that other papers had been quite successful with snappy copy. In 1875, when four murderers made some pious comments just before being hanged, the *Chicago Times* ran the immortal headline, "JERKED TO JESUS." Pulitzer followed suit. He stopped running such stupefying *World* heads as "AFFAIRS AT ALBANY" and "BENCH SHOW OF DOGS" and led off with "MADDENED BY MARRIAGE" and "SCREAMING FOR MERCY."

As he increased circulation Pulitzer revealed his genius at changing minds and selling papers simultaneously. For example, the *World* helped Grover Cleveland defeat Republican James G. Blaine in the race for the presidency in 1884, in part by loudly publishing an impolitic remark made by a Blaine supporter to the effect that the Democratic party had its roots in "rum, Romanism, and rebellion." New York state, with its sizeable Catholic constituency, went for Cleveland by a slim 600 votes, barely squeezing him into the White House with its 36 crucial electoral votes.

Within a year of Pulitzer's takeover, the *World*'s circulation passed 100,000—a number far short of his goal of a million but well worth celebrating. He had a 100-gun salute fired in City Hall Park and bought tall silk hats for all his employees. By the late 1880s the *World*, whose morning and evening editions were rich in advertising and sold more than 300,000 copies combined, had become the most profitable newspaper ever published. Pulitzer's income was about one million dollars a year, and he spent it on a yacht and houses in Maine, the Riviera, and New York—

still stoutly maintaining on his editorial page that luxuries and large incomes ought to be taxed.

Pulitzer's expenditure of energy cost him dearly. Although his physical courage was unquestionable, he suffered from nerves—the noise of crumpling paper, or even the sound of someone eating a piece of toast, drove him into agonies—and was treated for asthma, diabetes, headaches, insomnia, dyspepsia, and rheumatism. His eyesight became so poor that he began to stroke the faces of his wife and children as though trying to memorize them. On his doctors' advice he ceased editing the *World* and went abroad for a rest. In Constantinople in 1889, standing on a ship, he remarked, "How quickly it grows dark in this latitude." His companion said, "But it is not dark." "It is for me," Pulitzer replied. He had gone blind.

After 1889 the publisher, voyaging repeatedly to Europe, spent little time in New York. Contrary to his doctors' orders he continued to work. He managed the paper by cable, having each issue read to him and firing off detailed critiques. For personal services, he relied upon a staff of male secretaries—he preferred highly cultivated, soft-voiced Englishmen—who accompanied him everywhere. Among other duties they had the task of reading the master to sleep for his afternoon nap. When Pulitzer fell asleep the secretary would have to continue mumbling for as long as two hours—and if he once changed his tone, sneezed, or coughed, Pulitzer would awaken and berate him for a full 15 minutes.

In 1895 Pulitzer, whose vigor seemed only to increase with his illnesses, took a direct hand in U.S. foreign policy. A boundary dispute arose in South America between Venezuela and British Guiana (and hence England itself) concerning a tract of jungle that had been only vaguely surveyed. Citing the Monroe Doctrine, President Cleveland virtually demanded that the dispute be resolved on U.S. terms.

An unquenchable lust for battle arose—the New York *Sun,* one of the *World*'s rivals, said that anyone who did not want to fight England was "an alien or a traitor." In one of American journalism's finest hours, Pulitzer stood up

French Scientist and Explorer Discovers a Race of Savages with Well-Developed Tails.

NEW YORK, SUNDAY, DECEMBER 15, 1895.—COPYRIGHTED BY THE PRESS PUBLISHING CO., 1895.

The Missing Link.

THE HUMAN MAN-MONKEY WITH A TAIL

EXPLORER

Sunday supplements pioneered by Pulitzer had many trumped-up features. This creature was reportedly found by an explorer who was quoted in English and French to establish credibility— "to be certain that I was not the plaything of an illusion, I felt his tail (l'appendice caudal)."

THE WORLD.

ROUND THE WORLD WITH NELLIE BLY.

NEW YORK, SUNDAY, JANUARY 26, 1890.

PAGES 21 TO 28.

CUT OUT THIS GAME, PLACE IT ON A TABLE OR PASTE IT ON CARDBOARD AND PLAY ACCORDING TO SIMPLE DIRECTIONS BELOW.

THE WORLD'S GLOBE CIRCLER

ALL RECORDS BROKEN

SPEEDING ACROSS THE ATLANTIC

OVER A MILE A MINUTE

Manufactured news was a favorite method of selling papers. In perhaps the most spectacular of these promotional stunts, Pulitzer sent dashing lady reporter "Nellie Bly" (her real name was Elizabeth Cochran) around the world for the World. Racing against the record of the fictional Phileas Fogg in Jules Verne's novel Around the World in Eighty Days, Nellie traveled by sampan, jinricksha, burro, and train. The World kept its readers in a constant swivet with a storm of stories, pictures, and games, including the shake-the-dice race at right. When Nellie came panting back to New York, she had been on the road for only 72 days, 6 hours, 11 minutes, and 14 seconds, and had become far more famous than the notorious slowpoke, Phileas Fogg.

boldly against the general sentiment for war: "Does the determination of a boundary line in South America threaten . . . 'our distinctive form of government?' Merely to ask such questions is to expose the . . . preposterously inadequate nature of the war-threat which the president has fulminated." Pulitzer sent cablegrams to scores of British leaders, asking them to send him by return cable, collect, their thoughts concerning peace. On Christmas Day, 1895, the *World* ran a special front page headed "PEACE AND GOOD WILL" and featuring the British reply ("earnestly trust . . . warm feeling of friendship . . . so many years"). At this, most war promoters across the nation suddenly looked ridiculous.

In the mid-90s Pulitzer was challenged by young William Randolph Hearst, who came to New York and bought the *Journal*. Hearst admired Pulitzer and imitated his tactics; indeed, in one piratical swoop he hired away the entire staff of Pulitzer's Sunday paper, who strolled in a body from the *World*'s office to the *Journal*'s. Pulitzer, cabling an offer of more money, persuaded them to walk back; Hearst offered still more and the staff took another stroll, this time remaining at the *Journal* for good. Pulitzer quickly assembled a new staff but realized that he was facing a most formidable competitor.

Almost immediately Hearst began to publish ghastly tales of butcheries in Cuba, where Spain was attempting to maintain its colonial rule. Hearst's stories were largely fabrications, but the *Journal*'s circulation began to soar and, apparently, Pulitzer lost his head. He set out to compete with Hearst in sensationalism, and soon the *World* was printing: "The skulls of all were split to pieces down to the eyes. Some of these were gouged out. . . . The arms and legs of one had been dismembered and laced into a rude attempt at a Cuban five-pointed star. . . . The tongue of one had been cut out and placed on the mangled fore-

IT BREAKS ALL RECORDS.

The Net Paid Circulation of the
EVENING JOURNAL
Last Week Averaged
510,197 PER DAY.

THIS MEANS papers actually sold—all returns, free copies, office files and exchanges deducted.

THIS MEANS an average circulation of 50,000 per day MORE THAN the COMBINED CIRCULATIONS of

THE EVENING WORLD, The Evening Telegram, The Evening Post, The Mail and Express and The Commercial Advertiser.

THE POPULARITY OF THE EVENING JOURNAL IS OWING TO ITS BEING
A HOME AND FAMILY PAPER.

head. . . . The Spanish soldiers habitually cut off the ears of the Cuban dead and retain them as trophies."

Prose of that wild sort, repeated day after day by both papers, created an irreversible demand for war all across the nation. When the U.S. battleship *Maine* mysteriously exploded and sank in Havana harbor in February 1898 (a naval court of inquiry failed to fix the responsibility), Pulitzer and Hearst wasted no time in announcing their opinions: The wicked Spaniards had undoubtedly done it. When war was declared two months later, Pulitzer and Hearst were largely responsible for it, and both of them profited enormously. On the news of the *Maine*'s sinking, the *World* and the *Journal* topped a million in daily sales, and when Spanish-held Manila fell to Admiral Dewey, each paper sold about 1.5 million. It was a triumph of sorts, but the real verdict on this kind of journalism was passed by Edwin Godkin, the widely respected editor of the *New York Evening Post*, who said simply, "Nothing so disgraceful . . . has been known in the history of American journalism."

When the war ended, Pulitzer had repented of his attempt to scrimmage on Hearst's level. He summoned his editors and quietly discussed the state of the *World* with them. One of them summed up what the boss was feeling: "The great mistakes which have been made . . . have been caused by an excess of zeal. Be just as clever as you can. Be more energetic and enterprising than any other man if you can, but above all, be right." It was in this chastened mood that Joseph Pulitzer, having helped to create the new sensationalism, saw the old century pass away.

To build circulation Hearst treated the mystery of a dismembered corpse as a game with a prize. Later, his reporters caught the murderers.

NIGHT SPECIAL.

ZOLA'S "WIFE BEATERS"----READ IT TO-DAY.

NEW YORK EVENING JOURNAL

NIGHT SPECIAL.

NO. 5,566—P. M. NEW YORK, FRIDAY, FEBRUARY 11, 1898. PRICE ONE CENT.

EXTRA

BABIES KILLED BY SCORE

Twenty Bodies Have Been Recently Found in the Streets of Harlem.

POLICE AFTER SLAYERS.

Direct Attention to Midwives and Already One Arrest Has Been Made.

SHE IS HELD WITHOUT BAIL.

Harlem is to-day confronted with such another grewsome mystery of dead babies as recently aroused the Hoboken police.

Hardly a day in the last thirty has gone by that a dead baby has not been found in some doorway or alley.

Ever since the appalling accusations of wholesale baby murder were made against Mrs. Augusta Nack, the co-slayer of Wm. Guldensuppe, by her husband, Herman Nack, the police have been suspicious of the vocation of midwives.

An Important Arrest.

They consider as highly important the arrest and arraignment to-day of Mrs. Eva Gogansi, a midwife of No. 245 East One Hundred and Tenth street, who was held, without bail, to await the result of injuries to Mrs. Mary Ethel Gardner, upon whom she operated three weeks ago.

Mrs. Gardner is dying at her home, No. 325 West Thirty-seventh street. A consultation of physicians has been held, and at their instance Coroner Zucca has taken the woman's ante-mortem statement. She has

THE POLICE KEEP BRINGING THEM IN.
THEY ARE ABANDONED IN THE RAILROAD YARDS.

FOUND IN LONELY PLACES

AND DISCOVERED IN DARK DOORWAYS.

The Harlem police are convinced that a baby farm is in operation within their district. Twenty bodies of slaughtered babes have been found within the last month in doorways, alleys and secluded spots. A suspicious woman was seen at Park avenue and Ninety-eighth street carrying a small wooden box, which she threw under the "L" road. A policeman picked up the box and found it contained the body of an infant two days old. The scenes in the sketch show some of the discoveries of dead babies by the police.

Twenty Murdered Babies Found in Harlem Streets.

told of the treatment she received at the hands of Mrs. Gogansi, and if she dies the case will go to the Coroner's office and the midwife will be charged with murder.

Detectives on the Case

Detectives have been assigned to the case, and no efforts are to be spared to investigate it to its bottom.

Mrs. Gardner sought the services of the midwife three weeks ago, upon seeing her advertisement in a daily newspaper.

The criminal operation was performed and Mrs. Gardner paid the midwife $15. As the fee charge was $25, there was still $10 to be paid.

Woman in Critical Condition.

Soon after the operation Mrs. Gardner became suddenly ill. Dr. Conwell, of No. 144 West Thirty-second street, was summoned, and found the woman's condition serious. It became critical, and Dr. Conwell sent for Dr. Rockwood, of No. 240 West Thirty-fourth street, in order to hold a consultation.

The woman was then so ill, and death seemed a matter of so short a time, that the physicians sent hurriedly for Coroner Zucca to take her ante-mortem statement.

Told of Her Treatment

Although very weak, Mrs. Gardner disclosed all the details of her treatment by Mrs. Gogansi, and the arrest of the midwife was made imperative.

Captain Brown and Detectives Trojan and Mason, of the West Thirty-seventh street station, went to Mrs. Gogansi's house to-day and placed her under arrest.

She was not subjected to examination in Harlem Court.

Harlem Morgue Crowded.

The Harlem Morgue has never before had so many such infants in years. The police are mystified. Nothing presents itself as

Continued on Sixth Page.

ALLOWS $605,237 FOR THE TEACHERS.

Board of Estimate Fixes the Amount for Salaries and Other Expenses for January.

The Board of Estimate and Apportionment this afternoon allowed $605,237 for the Board of Education, covering expenses and salaries for January.

The Board heard Colonel Keatny on a proposition to renovate the brownstone building in City Hall Park for the use of the City Court. He agreed to put in new floors and elevators and to make other improvements for $15,000.

The bid was accepted.

THE DE LOME QUESTION

Washington, Feb. 11. — Will Hale sail?

BELIEVED TO BE TROLLEY ROBBERS.

Four Men Arrested on Suspicion of Having Murdered a Philadelphia Motorman.

Detectives Cronin and Brown this afternoon arrested four men in a Bowery lodging house who are believed by the police to be the highwaymen who on December 26 held up a trolley car near Philadelphia, shot the motorman and robbed the passengers.

The prisoners were taken to the Centre Street Court and were remanded. Philadelphia police will try to identify the men.

ABSOLUTE DIVORCE FOR F. L. COLWELL.

He Is Also Given the Custody of His Children—A $50,000 Verdict for Damages.

Justice Chase, in the Supreme Court to-day, granted Frederick L. Colwell an absolute divorce from his wife, Genevieve R. Colwell. He was also given the custody of their children, and all the papers in the case, as well as the testimony which was taken before Senator Jacob A. Cantor as referee, were ordered sealed.

The co-respondent named in the case is Dr. Charles A. Tinker. Some time ago Mr. Colwell, who is a stock broker, sued Dr. Tinker for damages in having alienated the affections of Mrs. Colwell. He was awarded a verdict of $50,000.

$5,000,000 for Klondike Claims.

Philadelphia, Pa., Feb. 11.—Kepner, of Seattle and Dawson City, has sold his Klondike claims on Bonanza Creek for $5,000,000 to the Reliance Mining & Trading Company, John Noble Welch, president.

LIGHT ON DREYFUS PLOTTING

Colonel Picquart Tells of Disregarded Evidence Against Esterhazy.

HANDWRITING RECOGNIZED

Zola Feelingly Replies to a Reflection of General Pellieux Amid Great Excitement.

WHAT M. BERTILLON DISCOVERED.

Paris, Feb. 11.—Colonel Picquart, while waiting in the corridor of the Assizes to-day to be called as a witness in the trial of Emil Zola, created an immense sensation by declaring that he had decided to disclose the whole Dryfus mystery in the witness box regardless of consequences to himself, the army and the country.

Pellieux's Shaft at Zola.

General Pellieux, who was the first witness of the day, testified that General Saussier, the former Military Governor, desired a public trial for Major Esterhazy, but General Billot, the Minister for War, ordered the trial be secret.

"Nevertheless," the witness added, "the court martial refused to keep the entire proceedings secret."

"If the members of the court martial," continued the General dramatically, "who spilled their blood on battle fields while others were no one knows where, had been heard here, they would have indignantly repudiated the accusations against them. I, their chief will be their mouthpiece, and I affirm that the court martial was regular."

There was a tremendous uproar and M. Zola flushed. When General Pellieux left the stand he rose and said:

Zola's Retort.

"There are several ways of serving France." His voice showed considerable emotion. "You, General, made your campaigns; but I will bequeath to posterity the

Continued on Sixth Page.

This Woman the Police Call a Second Mrs. Nack.

(Sketched from Life at the West Side Police Court To-day.)

Mrs. Eva Godorsi, a midwife, living at No. 325 West Twenty-seventh street, was arraigned in the West Side Police Court, charged with operating on Mrs. Mary A. Gardner. The police are investigating her record, with a prospect of startling results.

THIGH OF THE BODY FOUND.

NEW CLEW TO THE EAST RIVER MYSTERY.

$1,000 REWARD FOR SOLUTION.

Evening Journal Will Pay This for the Clearing Up of the Crime.

Questions to be answered and detective clews up to date:

WHO WAS HE?

Jean Lanereз?	George Farrell?
C. Swartschild?	Peter Smith?
T. Abrahamson?	—— ——?
Wm. McGarigle?	

WHY WAS HE SLAIN?

For Money?	By a Woman?
For Revenge?	In a Quarrel?
For Jealousy?	By a Maniac?

WHO KILLED HIM?

Nothing Known of the Identity of the Murderer.

HOW WAS HE KILLED?

Choked?	Crushed?
Shot?	Dismembered?

WHERE WAS HE KILLED?

Not more than a week ago. No one knows, but somewhere in the limits of New York.

A man's thigh was found floating in the East River at the foot of Pacific street, Brooklyn to-day.

Careful measurements taken by the Evening Journal showed at once that the limb was a part of the body of the murdered man whose trunk was at the Morgue.

These measurements were confirmed by Coroner's Physician Donlin and other experts when the thigh was brought to the Morgue this afternoon. The two parts fitted perfectly.

About thirty contusions were found, proving beyond doubt that the murdered man had engaged in a fierce struggle.

The body had apparently been disjointed by the use of a hatchet, pounded with a hammer.

The bone in the thigh was complete. The joints were disarticulated. The flesh was hacked. Then the joints were twisted and torn from the sockets.

The finding of the thigh has added a new and thrilling interest to the great murder mystery. For information leading to its solution the Evening Journal will pay $1,000 reward.

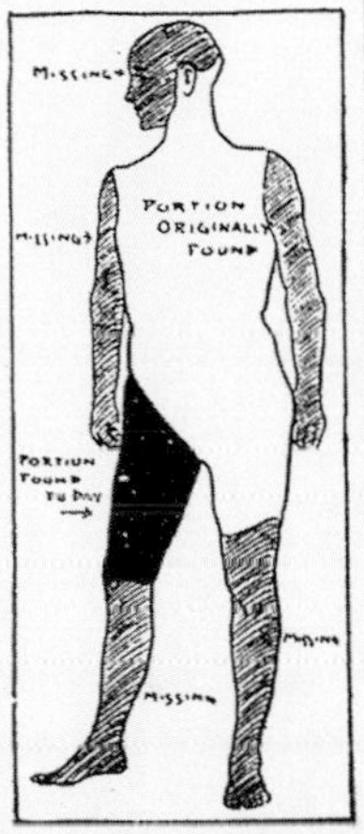
MISSING
PORTION ORIGINALLY FOUND
MISSING
PORTION FOUND TO DAY
MISSING
MISSING

Part of Leg Belonging to Mutilated Body Found in the River To-day.

The stump of a human leg wrenched from the hip and extending to the knee cap was found in the river to-day. It belongs to the dismembered corpse of the East River mystery. It is considered the most important clew to the identity of the victim. The shaded lines show the parts of the body still missing, and the solid black the part found to-day.

The right thigh of the murdered man whose trunk floated into the Roosevelt street ferry slip last Monday was found in the East River, at the foot of Pacific street, Brooklyn, to-day.

The thigh reached the Morgue at 1:35 o'clock. It was brought from Brooklyn in a baby's coffin and wrapped in a canvas covering.

It was placed in a closet in the dissecting room to await an examination by Coroner's Physician Donlin. No effort was made to fit the limb upon the body until Dr. Donlin had arrived.

DISCOVERY DRE WA CROWD.

At 7:30 o'clock this morning Joseph Morgan, a boatman, living at No. 75 Pacific street, saw an object bobbing up and down on the water near the shore. He drew it in with a boathook and found it was a man's thigh well preserved.

Morgan notified Policeman Ross.

The thigh was taken to the Fifteenth Precinct police station, at Emmett and Amity streets. Captain Michael Campbell at once notified Police Headquarters in this city, and detectives were sent over to confirm the suspicion that the thigh was a part of the body at the Morgue.

PARTS FIT PEBFECTLY.

Dr. Donlin arrived at the Morgue at 2 o'clock.

He at once began taking the measurements of the thigh. When he had finished he said:

"This is undoubtedly the leg of the trunk."

The scars, Dr. Donlin said, were post-mortem abrasions.

On the thigh he found about thirty contusions and bruises which were received before death. These were evidently made by pressure, as though the leg had been beaten or jumped upon.

The thigh was then joined to the trunk. It fitted perfectly.

"The last doubt is removed," said Dr. Donlin. "It fits as snug as a bug in a rug."

DISJOINTED WITH A HATCHET.

"From the appearance of the bone," said Dr. Donlin, "the murderers disjointed the leg by means of a hammer on the back part of a hatchet. They evidently found that the sharp edge of the hatchet was not equal to the purpose."

Dr. McAllister, Detectives Manion, Stransky, Webb, Chrystal and several of the medical staff of Bellevue were present.

The trunk had been carried into the autopsy room and placed on an operating table. It was a moment of suppressed excitement. All leaned forward eagerly as Dr. Donlin lifted the thigh out of the baby's coffin and fitted it to the trunk.

BODY TO BE PRESERVED.

After it was undoubtedly proved that the thigh was a part of the murdered man's body the limb and the trunk were taken into another room and placed in a preparation for preserving them.

Dr. Donlin said the scars on the thigh were received after death, and hence would not serve as means of identification.

Detective Sergeant Mannion said:

"I think that the remaining fragments of the body are at present floating around in the river.

OTHER PARTS WILL BE FOUND.

"The front part of the skull, the face and the missing ear, as well as the lower portion of the right leg, and all of the left leg not attached to the trunk will be found, I believe, within a few days.

"It is probable that marks for identification will be found on the other portions of the body."

Orders have been issued to the harbor police to keep a strict watch for any portions of the body.

A crowd, drawn by the report that the

$1,000 REWARD!

The Evening Journal will pay $1,000 reward for information, given to it exclusively, that will lead to the identification of the body found in the East River on Tuesday, and the conviction of the supposed murderer or murderers.

EXTRA.

(BY WIRE TO THE EVENING JOURNAL FREE [illegible])

DANGER OF RIOT IN PARIS

PARIS, Feb. 11.—At 4 o'clock the crowd outside the Palace of Justice blocked all the neighboring streets, extending to the Pont Neuf, [illegible] was closed by the police.

It became evident that a serious demonstration would [illegible] close of the session, and a large force of troops was summoned [illegible] the barracks. After the interruption of the sitting Colonel Picquart [illegible] testimony. "The interests of my chiefs," he said, "suddenly [illegible], and I was sent away on a secret official mission. This was after I [illegible] in pursuing the investigation despite the discouragements and [illegible] attitudes of my superiors."

Then there followed several genuinely French incidents. When [illegible] Picquart was confronted with several previous witnesses [illegible] did not agree with his in certain points, each reaffirmed his version, [illegible] dience giving loud expression to its sympathies on both sides.

REDMOND AMENDMENT OVERWHELMINGLY DEFEATED.

LONDON, Feb. 11.—In the House of Commons this afternoon during the debate on [illegible], Mr. Redmond taunted Mr. Dillon, the anti-Parnellite leader, with not having moved a similar amendment. He declared the [illegible] Nationalist cause was sacrificed to the maintainance of a Liberal alliance.

Mr. James O'Kelly, Parnellite, member for North Roscommon, seconded Redmond's motion. Sir William Harcourt, the Liberal leader, said that Mr. Redmond had asked the Liberals to repudiate the supremacy of the imperial Parliament which had been placed in the forefront [illegible] home rule bills with the consent of the Irish party. Mr. Redmond's amendment was rejected by a vote of 233 to 65.

EDGEMONT SMELTING COMPANY GOES UP.

TRENTON, Feb. 11.—A receiver was appointed to-day for the Edgemont and Union Hill Smelting Company, a South Dakota concern incorporated in New Jersey with a capital of $6,000,000. This is one of the [illegible] in which Cashier Quinlan is said to have invested the funds of the [illegible] Bank, of New York. The receiver is Savery Bradley, of Philadelphia.

MR. ACTOR GETS HIS TAXES REDUCED.

John Jacob Astor got his personal taxes reduced in the Tax Department to-day from $2,000,000 to $350,000. Mr. Astor admitted owning upward of a million dollars' worth of property, but said that he was already taxed on $750,000 worth on hisbotel.

MORE MEN WALKED THE PLANK.

Thirty-six employes of the Brooklyn Bureau of Buildings and Supplies were dismissed this afternoon.

WANTS TO RENT PIER

The New York and Mormouth Transportation Company [illegible] Dock Board to-day for the lease of Pier 1 for ten years at [illegible]. The pier is now rented to the Iron Steamboat Company.

RACING AT SINGERLY.

THIRD RACE—Earn, Crown, Wexford.

FOURTH RACE—Harry Bennett, Heck Jr., Quilla.

The Victorians

★

This porch in Oakland, California, was done up in late nineteenth century style.

"Who knows how to be rich in America? Plenty of people know how to get money; but not very many know what best to do with it. To be rich properly is indeed a fine art. It requires culture, imagination and character."

E. L. Godkin in *The Nation*

Too Much Is Not Enough

In the long peace that followed the Civil War, the wealth of Americans multiplied prodigiously. Railroad builders, copper barons, ironmasters, gold miners, bankers, stockbrokers, public utilities operators, and realty speculators joined war profiteers among the rich: by 1889, no fewer than 100 Americans could claim annual incomes of $1.2 million or more. In groping for culture to match their fortunes, many of these budding Brahmins fell victim to their untrained imaginations—and tastes. As a result, the era seemed for a time to be dominated by the conviction that nothing succeeds like excess.

In building new houses befitting their changed status, the Victorian rich hired architects who often mismated classic styles, endowing the offspring with cupolas, dormers, arches, and gimcrackery, as in the house on the opposite page. Erected with no concern for cost, such structures conspicuously lacked grace, but they provided a satisfying degree of comfort for their owners.

The interiors were stuffed with settees, divans, ornate tables, and armchairs. In these same rooms, the Victorians also tended to stuff themselves, giving elaborate dinner parties that ran 12 heavy courses or more. Eager to display their level of refinement, they strove to emulate the older civilization of Europe by punctuating their careful conversations with *au 'voirs* and *recherchés,* and avidly collected paintings and sculpture, good or bad, from abroad.

This extravagance characterized almost every other aspect of Victorian life. At weddings, the brides wore frothy, heavily detailed gowns *(left)*. In the theater, every hero was a prodigy of courage and a paragon of virtue. In politics, every opponent was a black-hearted scoundrel. In manner and morals, every living move an American might make was carefully prescribed in books of etiquette—and every dying move, too, for the arbiters of taste were very precise regarding the proper dress and attitudes for the era's elaborate funerals. Though some Americans found all this extravagant posturing to be nothing more than tiresome ego exercise, most would have agreed that Diamond Jim Brady epitomized the mood of the period when he said, "Hell, I'm rich. It's time I had some fun."

Typical of the ornate houses of the 1880s, this Portland, Oregon, residence is festooned with fretwork from porch steps to gable peak.

Overstuffed Rooms

Like nature itself, every prospering Victorian matron abhorred a vacuum in the living space of her home. Accordingly, she stuffed every room from fanlight to floor with an eye-popping collection of umbrellas and fans, plaster busts, wicker rockers, lamps and cushions, coat racks, china cabinets, small tables, and countless other knickknacks.

"Provided there is room enough to move about without walking over the furniture, there is hardly likely to be too much in a room," said one professional decorator. An amateur critic who thought otherwise was the novelist William Dean Howells, who acidly describes a typically furnished apartment in the excerpt below.

Even an outing to a California picnic ground, dominated as usual by the man of the household, requires a wealth of accoutrements.

Everything had been done by the architect to save space, and everything to waste it by Mrs. Grosvenor Green. She had conformed to a law for the necessity of turning round in each room, and had folding-beds in the chambers; but wherever you might have turned round she had put a gimcrack so that you would knock it over if you did turn. Every shelf and dressing-case and mantel was littered with gimcracks. The front of the upright piano had what March called a short-skirted portière on it, and the top was covered with vases, with dragon candlesticks, and with fans. The floors were covered with filling, and then rugs, and then skins; the easy chairs all had tidies, Armenian and Turkish and Persian; the lounges and sofas had embroidered cushions hidden under tidies. The radiator was concealed by a screen, and over the top of this some Arab scarfs were flung. There was a super-abundance of clocks. China pugs guarded the hearth. Some red Japanese bird-kites were stuck about in the necks of spelter vases, a crimson umbrella hung open beneath the chandelier, and each globe had a shade of yellow silk.

–A Hazard of New Fortunes, 1889

Ornate clutter fills to overflowing a Staten Island parlor (above) and a California girl's bedroom (opposite).

A Search for Elegance

For the Victorian woman, elegance of appearance surpassed almost all other aspirations, and her hair and her gowns were the chief means by which she tried to achieve it. In a still religious America, she heeded the New Testament dictum that "if a woman have long hair, it is a glory to her"; she never cut it, but in this period of primness, she also never let it fall unfettered to her waist. Instead, she piled it on her head *(top)* in the 1870s, tortured it into ringlets *(bottom left and right)* in the 1880s, and arrayed it to frame her face in the 1890s *(middle right).* In dress, she swathed her body in reams of silks and satins; up to 20 yards went into an afternoon gown like the one opposite.

Bustles like this one reigned in 1876 but eventually grew smaller, until the bicycle and the slim, athletic Gibson girl banished them altogether.

Bearded Wonders

The gods and heroes wear beards," proclaimed Robert de Valcourt, a Victorian. And the late Victorian man, determined to look both god and hero, sprouted an infinite variety of facial adornment. This hairiness was a marked departure. No founding father sported a beard; Uncle Sam wore none until 1858. Then beards and mustaches suddenly bloomed everywhere. Gold prospectors and fast-shooting marshals made them a mark of virility. Distinguished thinkers like Carl Schurz gave them an air of intellectualism. Finally, Abe Lincoln, growing a beard after a little girl said it might help his looks, established facial hair as a male status symbol of the era.

By the late 1890s, beards were waning again, but eastern dudes like this still sported the handlebar mustache popularized by westerners.

Dressing Junior

For small boys, the Victorian period posed a problem of identity and occasionally of self-defense. By nature, the normal youngster saw himself as Tom Sawyer, the footloose hero of the 1876 children's favorite, *The Adventures of Tom Sawyer*. And in fact he often was; the novelist Mark Twain had drawn his hero from memory.

But the mothers of many small boys preferred to recast their precious offspring as Little Lord Fauntleroy, a fictional, golden-curled goody-goody *(see the excerpt below)* who called his mamma "Dearest," wore spotless velvet suits, and precociously discussed world affairs with the grocer. As a result of the motherly fascination with the doll-like Fauntleroy, many unfortunate sons had to face the streets in starched white suits *(left)* and coiffed and dressed in the styles at right.

Naturally there were hoots and sneers from youngsters who had escaped such maternal excesses. And just as naturally, there were some hard-knuckled confrontations from which many a reluctant Fauntleroy emerged looking and feeling much more like the good, tough Tom Sawyer he really was in his heart.

He started in life with a quantity of soft, fine, gold-colored hair, which curled up at the ends, and went into loose rings; he had big brown eyes and long eyelashes and a darling little face. His manners were so good, for a baby, that it was delightful to make his acquaintance. When he was old enough to walk out with his nurse, wearing a short white kilt skirt, and a big white hat set back on his curly yellow hair, he was so handsome and strong and rosy that he attracted everyone's attention, and his nurse would come home and tell his mamma stories of the ladies who had stopped their carriages to look at and speak to him. His childish soul was full of kindness and innocent feeling.
–Little Lord Fauntleroy, Frances Hodgson Burnett, 1886

"He was so handsome and strong and rosy that he attracted everyone's attention."

Little Lord Fauntleroy, Frances Hodgson Burnett

No doubt abhorred but tolerated by the boys who were stuffed into them, the fancy shirtwaist at left and the fur-trimmed Fauntleroy suit above were sure to transform even the most mischievous Tom Sawyers into little darlings —at least until the photographer finally finished his work and mother permitted a change of attire.

The personifications of sugar and spice, 19 little girls in California treat their dolls to a tea party on a lawn in 1887. Such frolics were regarded as sound training for an era when most girls married young and spent the rest of their lives managing households that averaged five people.

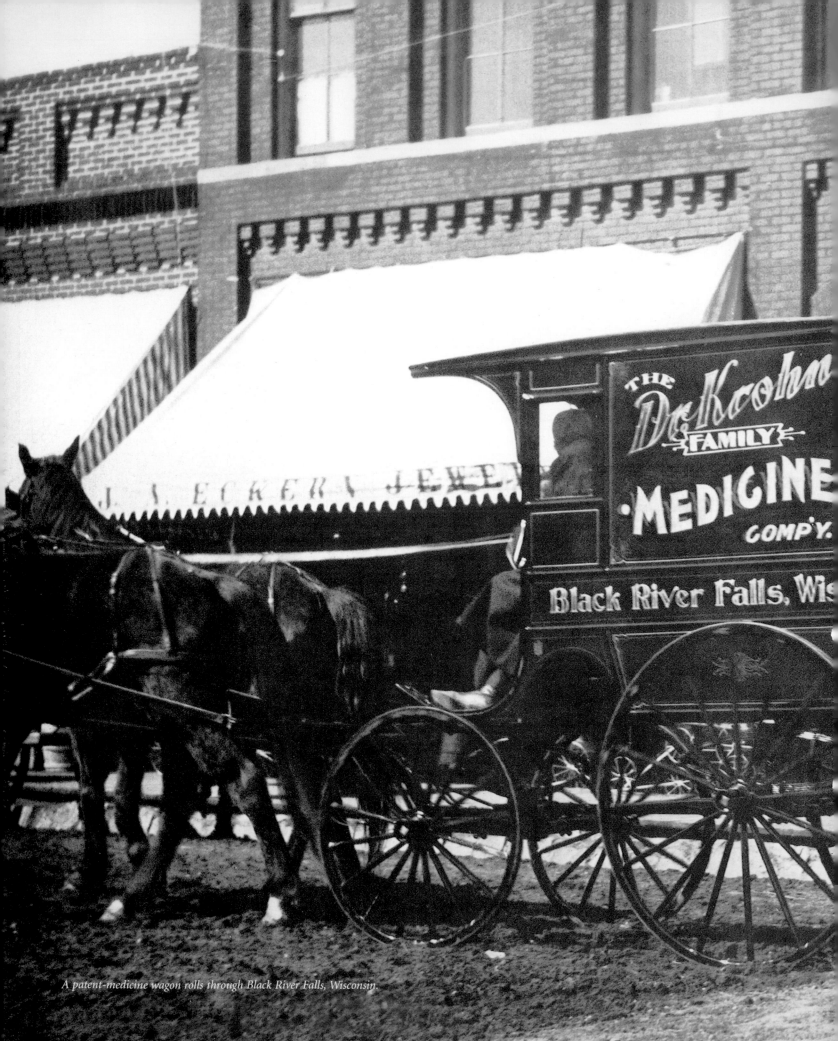

A patent-medicine wagon rolls through Black River Falls, Wisconsin.

Nostrums

★

A GULLIBLE NATION GETS CONNED

Many medications in the medical almanacs were as "gratuitous" as the mode of distribution.

"To draw the line nicely, and fix definitely where the medicine may end and the alcoholic beverage begin, is a task which has often perplexed and still greatly perplexes revenue officers."

Commissioner of Internal Revenue, 1883

Cure-alls with a Kick

When Johnny came marching home from the Civil War, he was likely at some time to have suffered from one of the so-called camp diseases—dysentery, malaria or typhoid. In those primitive medical times, he was also likely to have treated himself with a patent medicine such as Radway's Ready Relief, with which a noncom of the 8th Maine dosed some troops afflicted by typhoid and dysentery and claimed to have cured them. Johnny carried the home-remedy habit into civilian life, thus giving a great boost to the patent-medicine industry.

From 1870 to 1900, virtually every ailment had its own ready cure: indigestion (Hostetter's Celebrated Stomach Bitters), chronic fatigue (Ayer's Sarsaparilla), aching muscles (Barker's Liniment—"Joy to the World, Relief Has Come"). Most nostrum promoters presented their products as derivatives of America's popular folk-cure tradition: home-brewed remedies concocted by simple people with no need of fancy doctoring. Many patents were billed as Indian cures. One fast seller was the buffalo salve (for scabby scalps) ballyhooed by the braves in the touring Kickapoo Indian Medicine Company. But the most aggressive patent-medicine pushers used the new art of newspaper advertising *(pages 148-149)* to expand their markets.

There were, of course, two fundamental facts about the patent-medicine business. It was a fraud, and a dangerous fraud when it advertised nostrums for incurable diseases such as "consumption" (tuberculosis). Second, virtually all the most popular patents were loaded with hard drugs or alcohol, which ranged in quantity from a ladylike 18 percent in Mrs. Pinkham's Compound to a robust 44 percent in Hostetter's Bitters.

As early as the 1840s nostrum makers began giving away almanacs loaded down with patent-medicine advertising; by the 1890s some 30 million patent almanacs were being distributed annually to a population that numbered in the 60 millions. For rural families, these free almanacs were often the only new book of the year. The almanacs were splattered with overblown praise of the company's product, but along with all the huckstering was a potpourri of astrology, long-range weather forecasts, and jokes that entertained U.S. farm families throughout the year.

In 1898 a Junction City, Kansas, store sold a tonic whose 21 percent alcohol content kept it—and the consumer—from freezing in winter.

Home remedy makers were the most prolific advertisers in the United States during the 1880s. Nostrum peddling proved the best possible training

for copywriters in the nation's pioneer ad agencies; the products were basically so useless it took a clever man to make them seem worth buying.

Patent-medicine companies sent drugstores bushels of trade cards like these to use as free handouts. Card-swapping became such a big fad among

kids, who bedeviled druggists for the latest printings, that a popular song was written with the refrain, "Mister, got a pikcha card?"

Building the City

THE METROPOLIS TAKES SHAPE

Workers lay cable-car track in New York City, 1891.

The Magic Metropolis

We cannot all live in cities, yet nearly all seem determined to do so," journalist Horace Greeley commented in the late 1860s. Despite such warnings, in the next three decades the United States became a nation dominated by its urban centers. Between 1870 and 1900 the population of Detroit leaped from 79,500 to 285,700; Los Angeles from 5,700 to 102,400; Atlanta from 21,700 to 89,800; Philadelphia from 674,000 to 1,293,000.

Most of the new urban dwellers had come from the farm. Some had been pushed off the land by mechanized farm equipment that enabled one man to do the work of six. Others, particularly the young, were ambitious dreamers hankering to escape the monotony of rural life. In the city, they were joined by millions of immigrants, lured by the hope of finding America's streets paved with gold; five million entered the United States in the 1880s alone, and nearly all settled in cities.

Once there, many of the new arrivals faced a harsh awakening. Some immigrants found themselves stuffed into six-story tinderbox tenements; others were housed in dismal wooden row houses, thrown up right next to factories that smirched them with soot and smoke. Typhoid and cholera swept through such slums, and in 1880 the *Chicago Times* reported in disgust: "The river stinks. The air stinks. People's clothing, permeated by the foul atmosphere, stinks. No other word expresses it so well as stink."

Yet rising above smoke and filth, the American city of 1870 to 1900 also presented a facade as filled with magic as had been the dreams of the immigrants. Skyscrapers such as New York's Flatiron Building *(right)* soared up to 20 stories high, with electric elevators running miraculously up and down inside. Giant bridges reached across rivers more than 1,000 feet wide. Horseless trolleys crisscrossed cities at the incredible speed of 20 mph. Towns sparkled at night with the marvel of electric street lighting; Cleveland inaugurated the first municipal arc light system in 1879, and the Bijou Theatre in Boston followed by electrically illuminating a theatrical performance for the first time, with a dazzling array of 650 bulbs.

At the turn of the century, the largest, wealthiest, and most populous of these bursting urban centers was New York. And the description of that metropolis, offered in a phrase by a British visitor, was an eloquent summation of the U.S. city of the era: "a lady in ball costume, with diamonds in her ears, and her toes out at her boots."

"The thoroughfares are crowded, busy and bustling; and abounding signs of life and energy in the people are everywhere apparent."

British author Sir John Leng,
America in 1876

New York's Fuller Building, better known as the Flatiron Building due to its triangular configuration, nears completion in 1901.

A Giant Stride for Builders

"The contemplated work, when constructed according to my design, will be the greatest engineering work of this continent, and of the age."

John Augustus Roebling, on the Brooklyn Bridge

With the waters of the Atlantic, the Pacific, the Gulf and the Lakes commingled, emblematic of the Union effected by these mighty spans, I christen this structure the Illinois and St. Louis bridge, and invoke the blessings of the Almighty on it." So spoke Mrs. Julius S. Walsh, wife of a St. Louis railroad magnate on July 4, 1874, as she stood in a black grosgrain silk dress by the new 1,500-foot Eads Bridge spanning the Mississippi. Then she stepped forward and solemnly sprinkled the massive structure with the four waters from solid silver pitchers. In this genteel manner, America's first major steel structure *(inset)* was officially opened.

With its inauguration came a new era in city building. Until then engineers had been limited in the size of their structures by the brittle quality and weight of iron and masonry. But by the 1870s these materials had become inadequate as cities were pressing to expand outward and upward. A superstrong, flexible building material was needed, and it was found in the form of steel, just beginning to be mass produced.

The pioneer who took the first giant step with steel was Captain James Buchanan Eads, who masterminded the St. Louis bridge. Although Eads had never before attempted a bridge, he boldly drew up plans for a multispan structure of three cantilevered steel arches. While some engineers protested, Eads convinced others who counted, and his plan was accepted. On July 2, 1874, his bridge passed a spectacular test of strength as 14 locomotives weighing a total of 700 tons paraded across the sturdy, 520-foot center span. From then on, steel was the heart and spine of city building. In New York, engineer John Augustus Roebling designed the first suspension span to be supported by steel cables, the 1,600-foot Brooklyn Bridge *(right)*. The structure enabled Manhattan and outlying Brooklyn to unite in 1883 into one metropolis, thereby facilitating New York's growth to a population of 3.4 million by 1900.

Steel arches of the Eads Bridge begin to span the Mississippi River.

Four 16-inch steel cables and a narrow walkway reach across the East River to New York during construction of the Brooklyn Bridge.

Rise of the Skyscraper

Steel was also instrumental in the construction of buildings so tall they were called skyscrapers. William Le Baron Jenney pioneered such use of steel in 1884 when he designed Chicago's towering, 10-story Home Insurance Building *(below, left),* which was to be supported by a metal skeleton. Like James Buchanan Eads and John Augustus Roebling before him, Jenney endured the criticism of nervous doubters. (At the last minute one building commissioner insisted that the Home Insurance skeleton be reinforced with massive brick walls.) Nevertheless, within the decade bigger and better skyscrapers were rising over Chicago, St. Louis, New York, and Buffalo, topped in 1892 by Chicago's soaring 22-story Masonic Temple *(below, far right),* in its day the tallest building in the world.

Home Insurance Building,
Chicago, 1884

St. Paul Building,
New York, 1899

"He who is ready to admit that exigency of site gives some excuse for 'elevator architecture' will find a good deal to interest him in its practice in Chicago."

James Fullarton Muirhead, *The Land of Contrasts*, 1898

Union Trust Building, St. Louis, 1893

Masonic Temple, Chicago, 1892

A DEATH TRAP.

A New Lifestyle

Gentlemen will never consent to live on mere shelves under a common roof," a conservative New Yorker huffed as he contemplated a new phenomenon of city living—the apartment house. He was typical of the prosperous city dweller, who had always lived in a town house; to him, apartments were tenements fit only for the great unwashed. But by the early 1870s, in spite of a hustle of residential building, new private homes could not keep pace with the rise of city populations. Besides, town houses were becoming too expensive—even a modest one rented for $1,800 a year. Furthermore, the servants needed to maintain such an establishment were demanding salaries as high as $15 or $20 a month.

By 1870 it was apparent that a more compact and economical city dwelling unit was needed. It was provided, ironically, by a young New Yorker of impeccable family background, Rutherford Stuyvesant, who boldly opened New York's first apartment house, a five-story walk-up on East 18th Street. He patterned it after Parisian buildings, right down to the watchful concierge. And he described the apartments— six rooms and a bath that rented for $1,000 to $1,500 a year—with the fashionable-sounding name French Flats. Nicknamed Stuyvesant's Folly by skeptics, the building was nonetheless fully rented before it had even been finished. Within the next two decades a variety of taller and more elaborate apartment houses sprang up, including the eight-story Navarro Flats *(right)* and the nine-story Dakota *(page 167)*, the latter built at a cost of two million dollars. The Dakota boasted 15-foot ceilings, mahogany paneling, marble floors and nine hydraulic elevators—a necessity for the new mode of vertical living, but a horror to some of its passengers. By 1890, with 1.5 million people needing homes in Manhattan, apartment living was so well accepted that complaints about shortages began to be heard. "We often hear of specially desirable small apartments," wrote one periodical, "but when we attempt to find them they are like the will 'o the wisp."

The hazards of elevator travel in the 1880s were spoofed in cartoons like this one from The Wasp, *a western magazine.*

"The stoppage of the elevator car brings a dizziness to the head and sometimes a nausea at the stomach. The internal organs seem to want to rise into the throat."

Scientific American, July 12, 1890

The Navarro apartment house borders New York's Central Park.

Getting Around

By 1870 about a dozen American cities had populations of more than 100,000. Carriages and horse trams were choking the streets, and new ways had to be found to transport the growing mobs of urban commuters. One group of New York financiers proposed digging a tunnel eight feet in diameter the length of Manhattan from the Battery to the Harlem River. Through it they promised to move 20,000 people an hour in cars propelled by a windmaking machine. This ingenious notion died in merciful obscurity. A better idea was the cable car, introduced in San Francisco in 1873. In a secret trial at 5 a.m. on August 1, the motorman froze at the controls, fearing the cable would break, whereupon inventor Andrew Hallidie jumped in to take his place and triumphantly ran the car down Clay Street. The new machine became an instant success, and lines soon opened in Los Angeles *(left)*, Denver, Seattle, Omaha, and other cities. Though some continued to share the original motorman's qualms, most riders agreed with visitor Rudyard Kipling: "If it pleases Providence to make a car run up and down a slit in the ground for many miles, why shall I seek the reasons for this miracle?"

Even more miraculous was the electric trolley car, perfected by an ingenious engineer named Frank Sprague in Richmond, Virginia. Sprague also held a secret run. But the secret was poorly kept, and a sizable cluster of fascinated citizens was on hand to see the test trolley break down on a hill, from which it was ignominiously rescued by four mules. By February 2, 1888, however, a smooth-running system was ready for business and within two years 200 other cities had installed electric trolleys. By 1900 there were 30,000 cars with 15,000 miles of track, and the trolley had become an integral part of American life.

At a gala opening, the first cable car on Downey Avenue in Los Angeles glides by to the cheers of primly starched, flag-waving flower girls.

Diversity in the Marketplace

By the '70s American cities were teeming with people eager to buy the new factory-made goods—ranging from machine-produced shoes to canned meats—that were being turned out cheaply and in large quantities. As a result, retail sales methods began to change radically, the most striking innovations being the department store, the chain store, and the shopping center, all launched by city merchants. Perhaps the most far-sighted of these was Chicago's Marshall Field, who built an ordinary dry goods firm into one of America's first department stores *(left)*, with annual sales that reached $35 million by 1890. Field advertised directly to women in the *Chicago Magazine of Fashion, Music and Home Reading,* opened a bargain basement advertising goods that were "Less Expensive but Reliable," and in 1890, as a final come-on, opened a restaurant offering a variety of delicacies, served up with a complimentary rose.

Another smart dry-goods clerk who successfully appealed to women shoppers was Frank W. Woolworth. One morning in 1874 he took a tray of random items and marked them down to five and ten cents. By the end of the day almost all were sold. Thereupon Woolworth quit his job and opened a five- and ten-cent store in Lancaster, Pennsylvania. On the first day sales amounted to just $127.65. But only six years later he had a chain of 25 stores with annual sales of over $1 million apiece.

The city of Cleveland took the next logical marketing step in 1890, when it opened a huge arcade *(right)* that housed 112 jewelers, stationers, and leather goods shops, thus creating the nation's first true shopping center, where buyers could choose among the merchandise or simply enjoy a Sunday stroll, to the accompaniment of band music.

Four tiers of stores and offices line the 390-foot esplanade of a glittering arcade that was opened in downtown Cleveland in 1890.

> "It is a perfect bazaar. Not only is there a brilliant display in the windows of everything from Paris-imported bonnets to pink-satin boots, but the sidewalk is fringed with open-air stalls, heaped high with pretty things, many of them absurdly cheap."

An unidentified English visitor to New York's 14th Street

Marshall Field's is draped in flags for the Columbian Exposition.

Woolly denizens of Central Park's pastoral Sheep Meadow graze happily, some 25 years after the removal of the shanties, swill mills, and glue factories—not to mention the squatters and hogs— that once populated the region of the park.

Shanties such as these near Fifth Avenue and 91st Street often housed the same poor immigrant workers who were helping to construct the roads and town houses that would displace them.

Parks for the People

While a generation of brilliant pragmatists was solving the city's major construction problems, others with an eye on aesthetics and recreation focused on less strictly utilitarian matters. Those with a penchant for elegance concentrated on beautifying the urban milieu with heroic statues and triumphal arches, such as Philadelphia's gigantic bronze image of the city's founder, William Penn, which was hoisted in 14 sections to its permanent home atop City Hall's 548-foot tower, and the grandiose arch erected on New York's Fifth Avenue in 1899 to greet Admiral Dewey on his victorious return from Manila. A more significant contribution was that of the park builders, led by landscape architect Frederick Law Olmsted, whose avowed aim was to bring into the city, for all to share, "the beauty of the fields, the meadow, the prairie of the green pastures and the still waters." Despite such Elysian phrases, Olmsted was in fact a hard-driving realist influenced by the ideals of utopian socialism. He understood, for example, that in order to realize his dream of an open Sheep Meadow *(left, above)*, the area would have to be cleared of human habitation, just as the relentless northern expansion of the city inevitably forced the removal of numerous shanty settlements like the one near Fifth Avenue and 91st Street *(left, below)*.

By the 1870s, his Greensward plan had transformed 800 acres of rocky wilderness in the middle of Manhattan into a varied playground called Central Park. There were carriage roads, bridle paths, a zoo, a lake for boating *(pages 168-169)* and skating, and afternoon concerts where 40,000 people could listen from benches or sprawled on the grass. Inspired by Olmsted, other cities developed similar facilities and by 1880 there were 20 new park systems being constructed at a cost of nearly $50 million.

Skaters glide serenely in Central Park as the massive Dakota, allegedly named for its once-remote location, looms overhead.

Boys in New York, once largely bereft of recreational opportunities, enjoy a spirited toy boat race on the lake in Central Park, 1897.

Amusements and Pastimes

★

A WEALTH OF DIVERSIONS

The 1869 Cincinnati Red Stockings, baseball's first professional team, lounge comfortably as their photo is taken. The team was recruited and managed by Harry Wright (seated at far left), the British-born son of a prominent cricket player.

Standing Room Only

> "Mistress: Maggie, have you put fresh water in the goldfish bowl?
>
> Maid: No, they ain't drunk up what I gave 'em yesterday."
>
> Vaudeville skit, 1890s

Capitalizing on her eye-catching figure, Sylvia Starr became a popular performer on the burlesque circuit.

After the Civil War ended, Americans looked around and discovered that they were beginning to have both the time and the money to have some fun. Between 1870 and 1900, as the population rose from 39 to 76 million, annual income per capita went up from $779 to $1,164. Meanwhile, the work day for most citizens had decreased from 12 hours to 10 hours, and for many, Saturday was becoming a half holiday. With this combination of cold cash and leisure at their disposal, people began buying entertainment—going to shows, circuses, and sports events—with such exuberance that one shocked European visitor accused them of "gross sensuality" and said they were displaying a positive "mania for heaping up the elements of pleasure in excessive quantities."

When this mass quest for fun first got under way, the country had nothing that could be called commercial entertainment on a nationwide basis. Circuses still traveled by horse-drawn wagon and thus were restricted to regional or local tours. In the theater the producers promoted their shows in the old-fashioned manner, plugging thousands of forgettable dramas and providing headlines barely bigger than the copyright notice for the actors who could really draw the crowds. Racy burlesque shows *(right),* which were soon to become fixtures on the theatrical scene, were just beginning to gain acceptance by a more tolerant national audience. Sport was still afflicted by the ancient, upper-class stricture that the best athletes were gentlemen amateurs who would never play for pay and that any athlete who accepted money for his services was a scoundrel not worthy to be watched, much less admired. Thus the best-known teams were ostentatiously amateur and patently second rate; they played just for sport and exercise, before small, informal crowds, according to rules that varied from town to town.

By the end of the century that entertainment landscape had been radically altered. Shows of all kinds got bigger and gaudier, and so did the crowds. Burlesque barkers and minstrel-show posters bragged of larger casts than their rivals, and the biggest shows usually outdrew smaller ones. This compulsion to bigness reached a climax of sorts in Boston, where theatrical manager John Stetson found himself dissatisfied with the staging of a scene depicting the Last Supper. Considering the problem for a moment, Stetson quickly solved it to his own satisfaction: with only 12 apostles the stage was too bare. Turning to an assistant, the maestro roared: "I know what I want! Gimme twenty-four!"

De Vere's HIGH ROLLERS Burlesque Co.

HEIGHT 5 FT. 8 IN.
NECK 14
SHOULDERS 37
BUST 35
WAIST 32
HIPS 38
CALF 14½
LEN. OF FOOT 10
LEN. OF LEG 35
WEIGHT 151 LBS.

SYLVIA STARR
"THE AMERICAN VENUS"

WHO POSED FOR LINDSTROM'S FAMOUS STATUE "LIGHT"
SHE WILL APPEAR AT EVERY PERFORMANCE IN "VISIONS OF ART"
HER BEAUTY AND ENTERTAINMENT HAVE CREATED A SENSATION.

Something for Everyone

From the burgeoning array of theatrical entertainments, the one that emerged as the most popular was the variety show, a catchall that encompassed three similar productions. When a hodgepodge of songs, dances, comedy skits and specialty acts was performed in blackface, it was called a minstrel show. If it was peppered with blue humor and decorated with buxom ladies in revealing tights, it was burlesque. And if it was cleaned up for family consumption, it was vaudeville. Producers and performers switched freely from one type of variety show to another, and sometimes the choice between burlesque and vaudeville for a night's entertainment was made when a stage manager peeked out at the audience and spied a cop.

Such versatility brought little beyond applause to the variety performers. Their pay in the 1880s was $20 a week in the big cities and $15 a week on the road—a little more than the $12 a week earned by a first-rate plumber. To earn their pay troupers might have to visit seven towns in a week and perform five times a night; indeed, shows in the West sometimes went on until daybreak or as long as the customers at the bar, which often faced the stage, were still buying drinks.

Of course the variety show was not the only form of entertainment available to the avid theatergoer. A few top performers of the legitimate stage such as Ada Rehan and John Drew attracted enthusiastic audiences to the theatrical classics. In 1894, William Gillette's *Too Much Johnson* stayed on Broadway for 216 performances. Melodramas, crafted with clear-cut lessons for the morally hard of hearing and populated with virtuous heros and dastardly villains, were a staple as well. Even the lowly minstrel show—now rightly viewed as a bizarre exercise in racist condescension—grew into a wildly popular extravaganza, with shows like Primrose and West's *(pages 176-177)* featuring full-sized orchestras and dozens of song-and-dance men decked out in elegant attire. The message from the promoters and impresarios of the era was clear: If you couldn't find a form of entertainment to your liking, you simply weren't looking hard enough.

First lady of the legitimate stage, Ada Rehan played 200 roles, her greatest being in The Taming of the Shrew in 1887.

Popular melodramas included For Her Children's Sake (right) and The Prisoner of Zenda (left), which ran for 112 performances in New York in 1895 and then moved to new triumphs in the sticks, where actors sometimes played 14 towns in as many days.

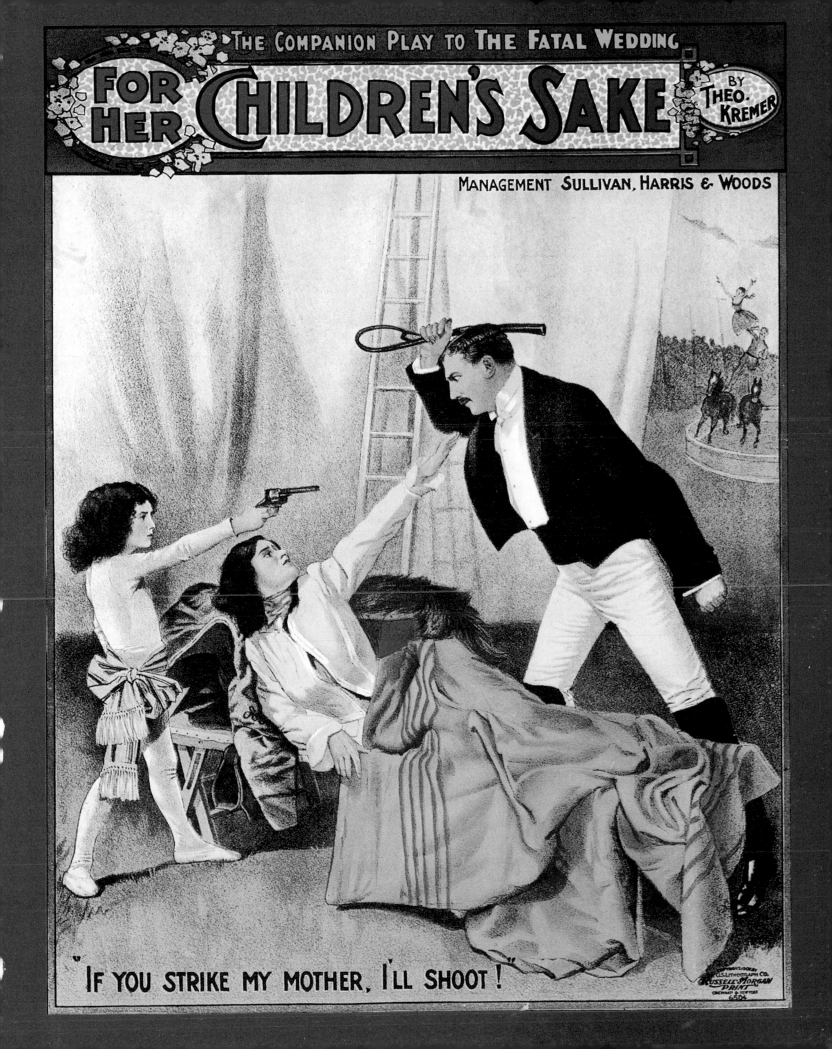

Brassy artists in the Adamless Eden shows took time out between their bawdy burlesque routines to dance with the cowboys at 50 cents a whirl.

By 1894 the Primrose and West minstrel show was one of the most successful large-scale productions. It was also one of the boldest, presenting black and white performers on the stage with equal billing.

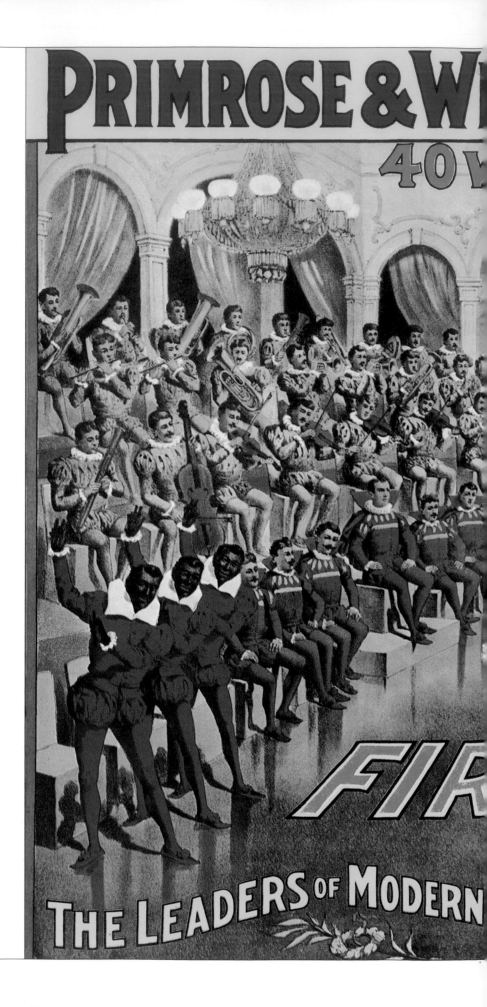

Basketball inventor James Naismith holds the peach basket and ball that were used in the early form of his game.

A Sporting Nation

Many of the sports that were to dominate the scene in the century to come were barely visible on the horizon. Football was still almost exclusively a college and club sport, though some historians consider the match between the Pittsburgh and Allegheny athletic clubs in 1892 the first professional game, since Allegheny officials paid former Yale star Pudge Heffelfinger the then princely sum of $500 to compete for them. Basketball was hatched in December 1891 from the fertile imagination of teacher James Naismith, who needed a means to divert his restive charges at the YMCA Training School in Springfield, Massachusetts, during the dark days of winter. "Those boys," Naismith would remark later, "simply would not play drop the handkerchief!"

Other sports began to reach a truly national audience for the first time. Boxing, greatly aided by the popularity of heavyweight champion John L. Sullivan, drew sellout crowds and avid readers to newspaper accounts of its bouts. Sullivan reigned from 1882 to 1892 as the last champion in boxing's bareknuckle era. His defeat on September 7, 1892, to the much smaller Jim Corbett—Sullivan weighed in at 212 pounds to Corbett's 178—was in part due to the fact that padded gloves were mandated for the first time, blunting Sullivan's clear advantage in power. Sheer exhaustion

The 1895 Cornell football squad was more impressive in its team photo than on the field, winning only three of eight games.

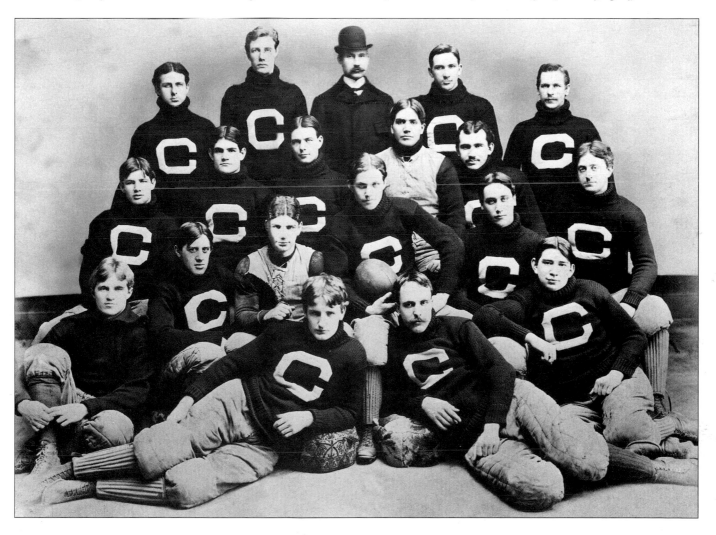

surely played a role as well; the two fighters battled through 21 rounds in the sweltering heat of New Orleans.

Thoroughbred horse racing also gained a foothold on the nation's affections. The sport's premier event, the Kentucky Derby, had its first running on May 17, 1875, and was won by Aristides, ridden by Oliver Davis, one of a slew of talented black jockeys who dominated early horse racing before Jim Crow rules forced them to ply their trade in Europe.

As promoters began profiting from the new money and leisure time available to many Americans, the public's distaste for professional athletics was brushed aside. Baseball led the way in 1869, when the Cincinnati Red Stockings fielded the first professional team, whose mercenaries earned up to $1,400 a season while proving that any pro could beat the pants off a gentleman and put on a good show doing it. On a 12,000-mile cross-country tour, playing against amateur clubs, the Red Stockings won 64 games without a loss and drew crowds of 3,000 and more. Other clubs joined the play-for-pay movement, and by 1876 the leading teams had formed the National League of Professional Baseball Clubs, which set up strict rules for its members. Rivalries grew between cities. Heroes such as Providence's Charlie (Old Hoss) Radbourne helped draw as many as 20,000 fans at 50 cents a head for games against Philadelphia, Cleveland and Buffalo. In 1886 *Harper's* announced, "The fascination of the game has seized upon the American people, irrespective of age, sex or other condition."

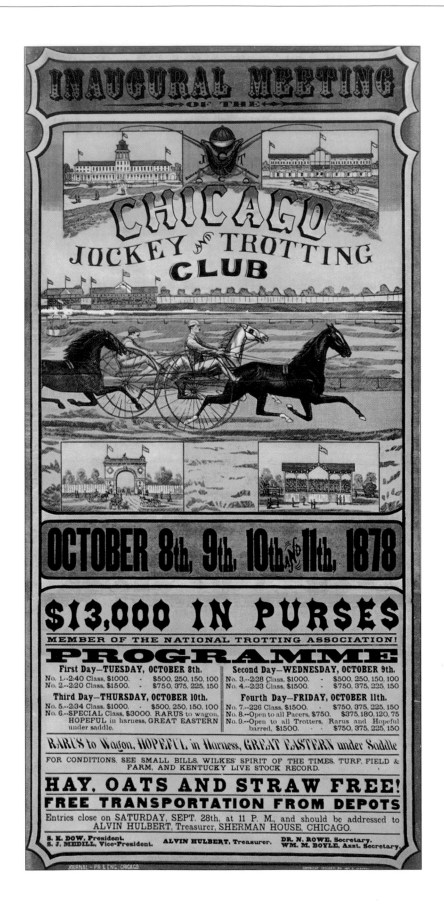

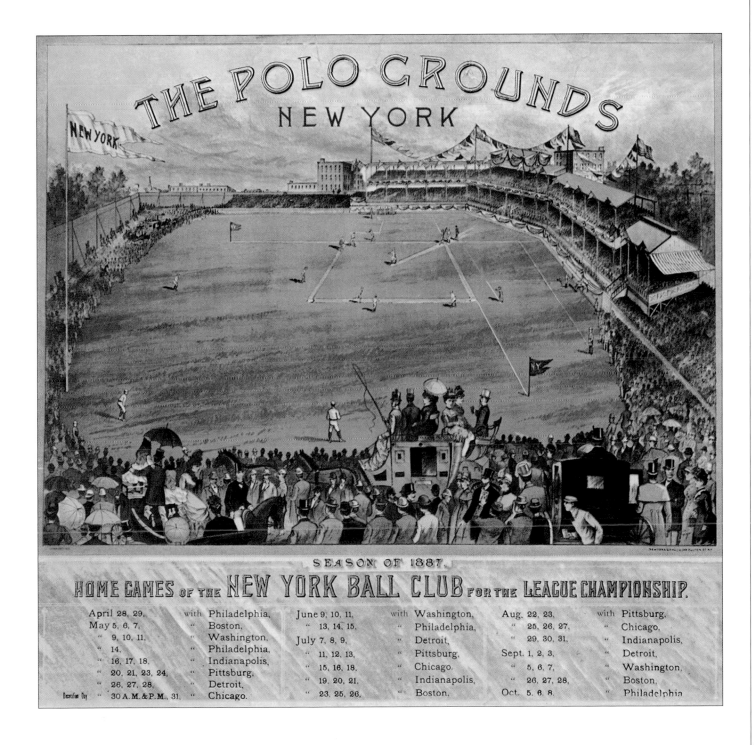

THE POLO GROUNDS
NEW YORK

NEW YORK

SEASON OF 1887.
HOME GAMES OF THE NEW YORK BALL CLUB FOR THE LEAGUE CHAMPIONSHIP.

April 28, 29,	with Philadelphia,	June 9, 10, 11,	with Washington,	Aug. 22, 23,	with Pittsburg,
May 5, 6, 7,	" Boston,	" 13, 14, 15,	" Philadelphia,	" 25, 26, 27,	" Chicago,
" 9, 10, 11,	" Washington,	July 7, 8, 9,	" Detroit,	" 29, 30, 31,	" Indianapolis,
" 14,	" Philadelphia,	" 11, 12, 13,	" Pittsburg,	Sept. 1, 2, 3,	" Detroit,
" 16, 17, 18,	" Indianapolis,	" 15, 16, 18,	" Chicago,	" 5, 6, 7,	" Washington,
" 20, 21, 23, 24,	" Pittsburg,	" 19, 20, 21,	" Indianapolis,	" 26, 27, 28,	" Boston,
Decoration Day " 30 A. M. & P.M., 31,	" Detroit, Chicago.	" 23, 25, 26,	" Boston,	Oct. 5. 6. 8.	" Philadelphia

In the entertainment boom that followed the Civil War, trotting races and baseball became the favorite spectator sports. Countless new trotting tracks were built all over the country, and one of them, the Chicago Driving Park (left) promptly drew a record crowd of 35,000. In baseball many a club could hardly cope with the soaring attendance. A new team called the New Yorks, soon to be rechristened the Giants, began playing in a 6,000-seat polo stadium in 1883 that was inundated by crowds of 12,000 and more. The overflow had to sit in carriages or stand in the outfield (above). A second and larger Polo Grounds was built in time for the 1891 season. There, only three years later, the Giants drew 400,000 fans for the season, a National League attendance record.

The Big Top Goes Big Time

The circus, like every other form of popular entertainment, had its share of empire-builders whose genius at promotion and expansion extended into outright rascality. One promoter, Adam Forepaugh, came honestly to the ownership of his circus but then stopped at nothing to pull crowds into his big tent. In 1884, when he learned that P. T. Barnum's circus had imported a $75,000 white elephant, Forepaugh promptly created another with a bucket of whitewash; then he printed up scurrilous handbills describing Barnum's beast as a "rank fraud."

Such slander aroused little sympathy for Phineas Taylor Barnum, whom everyone knew to be the brassiest faker of them all. Barnum once exhibited an elderly black woman as George Washington's nurse. (She would have had to have been at least 120 years old.) He even made a fake of a fake, exhibiting a plaster replica of the so-called Cardiff Giant, itself a carved stone phony being shown in upstate New York as the petrified remains of a primitive man. Such shenanigans were not limited to the larger operations, of course. The so-called dime shows, cheap circuses that worked the routes that were too remote for the big-tent

operators, also inevitably included several freaks of dubious authenticity.

However, as Barnum himself often and arrogantly declared, "There's a sucker born every minute." His circus grossed $400,000 in its first season, 1871. Three years later, after his greatly enlarged show had become the first circus to travel nationwide by railroad car, Barnum's gate receipts—50 cents each from about 20,000 customers a day—totaled roughly double his enormous operating costs of $5,000 a day.

No "human curiosities" were too bizarre to be exhibited—or faked—by Phineas T. Barnum (opposite), whose side-show performers helped make him the most successful circus operator of all.

Barnum & Bailey poster, 1898

The Greatest Showman on Earth

In 1883 the remote cow town of Omaha, Nebraska, was treated to the grand opening of a show that would reign as America's favorite for two decades. It was Buffalo Bill Cody's Wild West, and the locals gladly paid the 50-cent admission to see its famous star. Virtually every American knew of Cody: buffalo hunter, Pony Express rider, U.S. Cavalry scout, and professional actor—all this by the age of 37. Cody gave the Nebraskans their money's worth with a cast of trail-hardened cowboys putting on a dazzling display of stunt riding, fancy roping, and deadeye marksmanship. Cody himself topped them all with rifle and shotgun, hitting dozens of small glass balls while running or riding at full tilt.

The show set attendance records across America and throughout Europe. Eighty-three thousand people bought tickets in one day in London; and during a full, five-month season more than a million people turned up to watch Buffalo Bill do his stuff.

As producer, Cody steadily improved the quality of his troupe. In 1885 he took on as sharpshooter a comely young woman, Mrs. Phoebe Ann Butler, and gave her star billing as Annie Oakley, "Little Sure Shot." His most unusual talent catch was Sitting Bull, the Sioux chieftain whose braves had defeated the troops of General George Custer at Little Bighorn in 1876. The warrior chief signed on in 1885 for a $125 bonus and $50 a week, much of which he gave away to the poor urchins who hung around the show. When, at tour's end, Sitting Bull went back to his people, Bill gave his friend a rare prize: a performing horse that went into its act when a gun was fired.

To Cody's sorrow, he had not seen the last of that gift horse. In 1890, when Sitting Bull's Sioux were allegedly growing warlike on their Dakota reservation, a troop of Indians, recruited by the government, went to arrest the great chief. Sitting Bull refused to leave his people, and in the ensuing skirmish he was shot dead. Meanwhile the trick horse, at the cue of gunfire, kept rearing and pawing the air, convincing the Indians that the fallen chief's spirit had entered its body. Masterless but unharmed, the beast was returned to Cody to perform again in the Wild West show.

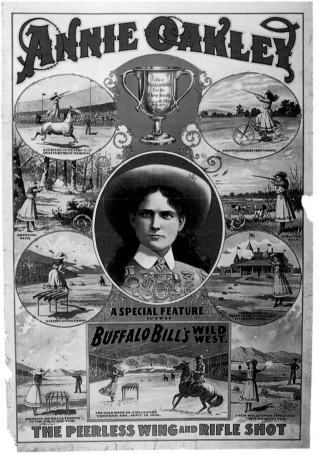

Cody never let his ego stand in the way of doing whatever was necessary to promote stars such as Annie Oakley (above).

Buffalo Bill and Sitting Bull pose (opposite) in 1886 during the chief's days with the Wild West show; four years later he would be killed.

The cast of Buffalo Bill's Wild West spectacular goes through its paces in an appearance in Omaha, Nebraska. The show was the nineteenth century's most popular: 41,448 saw a single performance in Chicago in 1884.

ACKNOWLEDGMENTS

The editors of this book wish to thank the following individuals and institutions for their valuable assistance in the preparation of this volume:
Frank Aydelotte and Jane Riss, University of Kansas; Frances Barger, *The Dallas Morning News*; Lawrence Belles and Mikel Darling, Evanston Historical Society, Evanston, Illinois; Amelia D. Bielaski, Curator, Smith-Telfer Collection, New York State Historical Association, Cooperstown, New York; Larry Booth, Director, Historical Collection, Title Insurance and Trust Company, San Diego; Nellie C. Carico, U.S. Geological Survey; Dr. Edwin H. Carpenter, Western Americana Bibliographer, Henry E. Huntington Library and Art Gallery, San Marino, California; Harry Collins, Brown Brothers, New York; John Cumming, Director, Clarke Historical Library, Central Michigan University, Mt. Pleasant; Virginia Daiker and Mrs. Elena Millie, Prints and Photographs Division, Library of Congress; Mrs. Alice Dalligan, Curator of Manuscripts, Burton Historical Collection, Detroit Public Library; Eugene Decker and Robert Richmond, Kansas State Historical Society, Topeka, Kansas; Mrs. Evelyn Draper, Archivist, Rollins College, Winter Park, Florida; Wilson Duprey, Curator of Prints, and James Gregory, Librarian, The New York Historical Society, New York; Barbara Friedman, Photographs and Maps Librarian, Oregon Historical Society, Portland; Dr. Thomas H. Gandy, Natchez, Mississippi; Woodrow Gelman, Nostalgia Press, Malverne, New York; Dorothy Gimmestad, Assistant Head, AudioVisual Library, Minnesota Historical Society, St. Paul; Mrs. Jennifer Goldsborough, The Society for the Preservation of New England Antiquities, Boston; Sinclair Hitchings and Mrs. Nancy Davidson, Print Department, Boston Public Library; Lowell Hocking, Director, Jacksonville Museum, Jacksonville, Oregon; Daniel W. Jones, Special Projects, NBC, New York; Alison Kallman, New York; Mrs. Jessie Kincheloe, Historical Picture Collection, Title Insurance and Trust Co., Los Angeles; Charlotte LaRue, John Noble and James Strobridge, Museum of the City of New York; Ellen Leiman, Little Meadow, Pennsylvania; Louisiana State Museum, New Orleans; John M. Cahoon, History Division, Los Angeles County Museum of Natural History; Mrs. Elsa B. Meier, Acquisitions Archivist, Louisiana State University Library, Baton Rouge; Harriett C. Meloy, Acting Librarian, Montana Historical Society, Helena; Allen Morris, Florida State Pictorial Archivist, Chief Clerk of the House, Tallahassee; Mrs. Irene Simpson Neasham, Director, Wells Fargo Bank History Room, San Francisco; Sol Novin, Culver Pictures, New York; George O'Neil, Director of Public Relations, Pinkerton's Inc., New York; Bob Parkinson, Circus World Museum, Baraboo, Wisconsin; Margot Pearsall, Detroit Historical Museum; Philip Pines, Curator, Hall of Fame of the Trotter, Goshen, New York; Robert C. Pettit, Curator of Collections, Dee Hermonie, Opal Jacobsen, Louise Small, Nebraska Historical Society, Lincoln; Mrs. Virginia Plisko and Mrs. Elizabeth Lessard, The Manchester Historic Association, Manchester, New Hampshire; Victor R. Plukas, Bank Historian, Security Pacific National Bank, Los Angeles; Davis Pratt, Curator of Still Photography, Harvard University, Cambridge, Massachusetts; Mrs. Elizabeth Rademacher, Michigan Historical Commission Archives, Lansing; Jack Redding, Baseball Hall of Fame, Cooperstown, New York; Martha and Ray Samuel, New Orleans; Sy Seidman, New York; Barbara Shepherd, Collection of Regional History and University Archives, Cornell University, Ithaca; Dr. John Barr Tompkins, Head of Public Services, Bancroft Library, University of California, Berkeley; Paul Vanderbilt, Curator, Elise Hall and Joan Severa, Iconographic Collection, State Historical Society of Wisconsin; Robert A. Weinstein, Los Angeles; Philip J. Welchman, Executive Director, and Dr. Elliot Evans, Curator, The Society of California Pioneers, San Francisco.

PICTURE CREDITS

The sources for the illustrations in this book are listed below. Credits from left to right are separated by semicolons, from top to bottom by dashes.

Cover and dust jacket: Corbis-Bettmann; Hulton Getty/Liaison; Hulton Getty/Liaison; Brown Brothers; Brown Brothers; Library of Congress; Culver Pictures—Solomon D. Butcher Collection, Nebraska State Historical Society. **6, 7:** Union Pacific Railroad. **8, 9:** Courtesy of the Bancroft Library, University of California, Berkeley. **10, 11:** Museum of the City of New York. **12, 13:** Library of Congress. **14, 15:** Joe Clark, owned by the Henry Ford Museum. **16, 17:** San Diego Historical Society. **18, 19:** The Manchester Historic Association, New Hampshire. **20, 21:** Brown Brothers. **22, 23:** The Bettmann Archive. **24:** Hulton Getty/Liaison—Library of Congress. **25:** Chicago Historical Society. **26, 27:** Colorado Historical Society. **28:** Brown Brothers. **29:** Corbis-Bettmann—Brown Brothers—Hall of Electrical History, Schenectady Museum. **30, 31:** Haynes Foundation, Bozeman, Montana; Hulton Getty/Liaison. **32:** Corbis-Bettmann—Brown Brothers. **33:** Miriam & Ira D. Wallach Division of Art, Prints & Photographs, The New York Public Library. **34:** Corbis-Bettmann. **35:** Culver Pictures. **36, 37:** Corbis-Bettmann. **38, 39:** Division of Manuscripts, University of Oklahoma Library. **41:** Denver Public Library, Western Collection. **42:** Library of Congress—Western History Department, Denver Public Library. **43:** Haynes Foundation, Bozeman, Montana. **44, 45:** Montana Historical Society, Helena. **46, 47:** Division of Manuscripts, University of Oklahoma Library. **48:** Kansas State Historical Society. **49:** Charles Phillips, courtesy Smithsonian Institution. **50, 51:** Library of Congress. **52:** U.S. Geological Survey Records Photo No. 57-HS-566 in the National Archives. **53:** U.S. Geological Survey Records Photo No. 57-HS-997 in the National Archives. **54, 55:** Minnesota Historical Society. **56, 57:** Haynes Foundation, Bozeman, Montana. **58:** Haynes Foundation, Bozeman, Montana. **59:** University of Washington Library, Special Collections. **60, 61:** Montana Historical Society, Helena. **63:** Minnesota Historical Society. **64, 65:** Wells Fargo Bank History Room, San Francisco; Helen Greenway, courtesy Library of Congress. **66, 67:** Wells Fargo Bank History Room, San Francisco. **68, 69:** Brown Brothers. **70, 71:** Minnesota Historical Society. **72:** Pinkerton's Inc.—Helen Greenway, courtesy Pinkerton's Inc. **73:** Pinkerton's Inc. **74, 75:** Frances Benjamin Johnston, courtesy Library of Congress. **76:** Courtesy of The New York Historical Society, New York City. **77:** Courtesy Mrs. Earl Moore, Weston, Connecticut—Courtesy of The New York Historical Society, New York City—State Historical Society of Wisconsin. Quotations courtesy Sy Seidman. **78:** Paulus Leeser, courtesy John Noble, New York; Paulus Leeser, courtesy Sy Seidman—Jacksonville Museum, Oregon. **79:** Paulus Leeser, courtesy Sy Seidman—Joe Clark, courtesy Detroit Historical Museum; Travis County Collection, Austin Public Library, Texas—Evanston Historical Society, Evanston, Illinois; Paulus Leeser, courtesy John Noble, New York; Paulus Leeser, courtesy Sy Seidman. **80:** Paulus Leeser, courtesy Museum of the City of New York; Paulus Leeser, courtesy John Noble, New York—Paulus Leeser, courtesy Sy Seidman—Paulus Leeser, courtesy John Noble, New York; Paulus Leeser, courtesy John Noble, New York. **81:** Joe Clark, courtesy Detroit Historical Museum—Paulus Leeser, courtesy John Noble, New York. **82:** Paulus Leeser, courtesy Sy Seidman—Evanston Historical Society, Evanston, Illinois—Paulus Leeser, courtesy Sy Seidman; Paulus Leeser, courtesy Sy Seidman. Quotations courtesy *The Dallas Morning News.* **83:** State Historical Society of Wisconsin—Chicago Historical Society; Paulus Leeser, courtesy Museum of the City of New York. Quotations courtesy Historical Society of Pennsylvania. **84:** Paulus Leeser, courtesy Sy Seidman—Paulus Leeser, courtesy John Noble, New York. **85:** Frances Benjamin Johnston, courtesy Museum of Modern Art—Paulus Leeser, courtesy Culver Pictures. Quotations courtesy Presbyterian Historical Society, Philadelphia, Pennsylvania. **86:** Sy Seidman—Joe Clark, courtesy Detroit Historical Museum; Joe Clark, courtesy Detroit Historical Museum—Joe Clark, courtesy Detroit Historical Museum. **87:** Paulus Leeser, courtesy Museum of the City of New York. **88, 89:** Florida State University Library. **90:** Culver Pictures; Culver Pictures. **91:** The Byron Collection, Museum of the City of New York. **92, 93:** Brown Brothers. **94, 95:** Courtesy of The New York Historical Society, New York City; Buffalo and Erie County Historical Society, Buffalo, New York. **96, 97:** The Massillon Museum, Massillon, Ohio. **98, 99:** Oregon Historical Society. **100:** From *The Life and Adventures of Nat Love,* published by Arno Press and *The New York Times* (1968); Courtesy of the Bancroft Library, University of California, Berkeley. **101:** The Huffman Pictures, Miles City, Montana; Florida State University Library. **102, 103:** The Huntington Library, San

BIBLIOGRAPHY

Bartlett, Richard A. *Great Surveys of the American West.* University of Oklahoma Press, 1962.

Beer, Thomas. *The Mauve Decade.* Alfred A. Knopf, 1926.

Bishop, Morris. *A History of Cornell.* Cornell University Press, 1962.

Brown, Dee. *The Year of the Century: 1876.* Charles Scribner's Sons, 1966.

Carson, Gerald. *One for a Man, Two for a Horse.* Doubleday & Co., 1961.

Carson, Gerald. *The Polite Americans.* William Morrow & Co., 1966.

Dorf, Philip. *The Builder: A Biography of Ezra Cornell.* The Macmillan Co., 1952.

Cubberley, Ellwood P. *Public Education in the United States.* Houghton Mifflin Co., 1947.

Dillon, Richard. *Wells Fargo Detective: The Biography of James B. Hume.* Coward-McCann, Inc., 1969.

Dulles, Foster Rhea. *America Learns to Play.* Appleton-Century Company, Inc., 1940.

Fox, Charles P., and Tom Parkinson. *The Circus in America.* Country Beautiful, 1969.

Glaab, Charles N., and A. Theodore Brown. *A History of Urban America.* The Macmillan Co., 1967.

Holbrook, Stewart H. *The Golden Age of Quackery.* The Macmillan Co., 1959.

Horan, James D., and Paul Sann. *Pictorial History of the Wild West.* Crown Publishers, Inc., 1954.

Horan, James D. *Desperate Men: Revelations from the Sealed Pinkerton Files.* G. P. Putnam's Sons, 1949.

Kouwenhoven, John A. *The Columbia Historical Portrait of New York.* Doubleday and Co., Inc., 1953.

Leonard, Irving A. *When Bikehood was in Flower.* Bearcamp Press, 1969.

Lewis, Oscar. *San Francisco: Mission to Metropolis.* Howell-North Books, 1966.

Loomis, Noel M. *Wells Fargo: An Illustrated History.* Clarkson N. Potter, Inc., 1968.

Mayer, Grace M. *Once Upon a City.* The Macmillan Co., 1958.

Mayer, Harold M., and Richard C. Wade. *Chicago: Growth of a Metropolis.* University of Chicago Press, 1969.

Morris, Lloyd. *Incredible New York.* Random House, 1951.

Nevins, Allan. *The Emergence of Modern America.* The Macmillan Co., 1927.

Palmer, Arthur Judson. *Riding High: The Story of the Bicycle.* E. P. Dutton & Co., Inc., 1956.

Pierce, Bessie Louise, ed. *As Others See Chicago.* The University of Chicago Press, 1933.

Randel, William P. *Centennial.* Chilton Book Co., 1969.

Ridge, Martin, and Ray A. Billington, eds. *America's Frontier Story.* Holt, Rinehart & Winston, 1969.

Ross, Marjorie Drake. *The Book of Boston–The Victorian Period 1837-1901.* Hastings House Publishers, 1964.

Russell, Don. *The Lives and Legends of Buffalo Bill.* University of Oklahoma Press, 1960.

Schlesinger, Arthur M. *The Rise of the City 1878-1898.* The Macmillan Co., 1933.

Silverberg, Robert. *Bridges.* MacRae Smith Co., 1966.

Still, Bayrd. *Mirror for Gotham.* New York University Press, 1956.

Sullivan, Mark. *Our Times: The United States 1900-1925, Vol. II.* Charles Scribner's Sons, 1939.

Swanberg, W. A. *Pulitzer, Vol. VIII.* Charles Scribner's Sons, 1967.

Tilden, Freeman. *Following the Frontier.* Alfred A. Knopf, 1964.

Wilson, Mitchell A. *American Science and Invention.* Barnes & Noble, 1960.

Young, James H. *The Toadstool Millionaires.* Princeton University Press, 1961.

INDEX

TIME®
LIFE
BOOKS

Time-Life Books is a division of Time Life Inc.

TIME LIFE INC.
PRESIDENT and CEO: George Artandi

TIME-LIFE BOOKS
PUBLISHER/MANAGING EDITOR: Neil Kagan
VICE PRESIDENT, MARKETING: Joseph A. Kuna
VICE PRESIDENT, NEW PRODUCT DEVELOPMENT:
Amy Golden

OUR AMERICAN CENTURY

EDITORS: Loretta Britten, Paul Mathless
DIRECTOR, NEW PRODUCT DEVELOPMENT:
Elizabeth D. Ward
DIRECTOR OF MARKETING: Pamela R. Farrell

Prelude to the Century: 1870–1900
Project Editor: Charles J. Hagner
Picture Coordinator: Betty H. Weatherley
Editorial Assistant: Christine Higgins

Design for **Our American Century** by Antonio Alcalá,
Studio A, Alexandria, Virginia.

Correspondents: Maria Vincenza Aloisi (Paris), Christine Hinze
(London), Christina Lieberman (New York).

Director of Finance: Christopher Hearing
Directors of Book Production: Marjann Caldwell, Patricia Pascale
Director of Publishing Technology: Betsi McGrath
Director of Photography and Research: John Conrad Weiser
Director of Editorial Administration: Barbara Levitt
Manager, Technical Services: Anne Topp
Senior Production Manager: Ken Sabol
Production Manager: Virginia Reardon
Quality Assurance Manager: James King
Chief Librarian: Louise D. Forstall

Prelude to the Century was produced by Bishop Books, Inc.,
New York City.

EDITORIAL CONSULTANT
Richard B. Stolley is currently senior editorial adviser at Time
Inc. After 19 years at *Life* magazine as a reporter, bureau chief,
and assistant managing editor, he became the first managing
editor of *People* magazine, a position he held with great success
for eight years. He then returned to *Life* magazine as managing
editor and later served as editorial director for all Time Inc.
magazines. In 1997 Stolley received the Henry Johnson Fisher
Award for Lifetime Achievement, the magazine industry's
highest honor.

Library of Congress Cataloging-in-Publication Data
Prelude to the century, 1870–1900 / by the editors of Time-Life
Books, Alexandria, Virginia.
p. cm. — (Our American century)
Includes bibliographical references and index.
ISBN 0-7835-5512-1
1. United States—History—1865–1898. 2. United States—
History—1865-1898—Pictorial works.
I. Time-Life Books. II. Series.
E661.P74 1999
973.8—dc21   98-54213
                                                CIP

Other History Publications:

World War II
What Life Was Like
The American Story
Voices of the Civil War
The American Indians
Lost Civilizations
Mysteries of the Unknown
Time Frame
The Civil War
Cultural Atlas

For information on and a full description of any of the Time-
Life Books series listed above, please call 1-800-621-7026
or write:

Reader Information
Time-Life Customer Service
P.O. Box C-32068
Richmond, Virginia 23261-2068